stitch!

Cath Kidston

stitch!

Cath Kidston

PHOTOGRAPHY BY PIA TRYDE

Quadrille
PUBLISHING

Introduction

The recent resurgence of interest in craft – and sewing in particular – has grown from a low-key trend into a much larger movement, and it now seems as if it's here to stay! It has been incredible to see just how many people, of all ages, are really enjoying making things by hand. A few years ago quite a few of my friends hadn't a clue how to sew on a button, let alone tackle any more advanced stitchery, so I find it very exciting that needlework has finally become mainstream.

My previous books, *Make!* and *Sew!* featured a wide variety of embroidery, appliqué and sewing projects inspired by my printed fabrics. When it came to planning *Stitch!* I wanted to take this exploration forward to the next level, and find a way of working these designs into step-by-step projects that focused on another traditional technique. Needlepoint tapestry was the natural choice. Thinking back to my childhood, tapestry was enormously popular, not least because it is so easily transported. My mother went everywhere with her sewing bag, and always had a project on the go, whether it was a cushion cover or a specs case. We also had an amazing rug, which my grandmother had made. She drew a picture of her house directly on to a large canvas and painstakingly filled in the outlines with carefully chosen coloured wools, using a variety of stitches.

What appeals to me about needlepoint is that the basics are very easy to learn and to put into practice, but the results are incredibly effective. Within a short time you can achieve a wonderful effect. Once I started translating my designs into charts, it immediately became apparent that

they would also work perfectly as counted cross stitch patterns. I had less experience in this medium, but soon discovered how much is possible... it is just as simple as needlepoint. All you need to do is to follow the chart and count your stitches as you go!

    I had to narrow my selection down to a final total of fifteen prints and motifs, but you'll find plenty of familiar old favourites, like the cowboy and little house, alongside some exciting new designs. Each motif is interpreted in two ways, in different colour schemes, and I was delighted to find just how versatile they are, and how well their delicacy and detail translates into both cross stitch and needlepoint. The cherry border for example, is a wonderful repeated cross stitch design, but a single motif in tent stitch makes an equally effective badge.

I hope I've made it easy for you to get started. All the technical background and stitches are detailed in the opening chapter so beginners will be able to tackle their first project with confidence and more experienced stitchers can brush up on their skills. The book comes complete with all the detailed instructions and charts needed to make the projects. Some pieces are quite quick to do, and easy for someone who is just starting out, whilst designs such as the floral chair seat and the striped rug may prove more a labour of love.

I am now completely hooked on my latest tapestry (very often in front of the TV) and I hope you will find needlepoint and cross stitch just as enjoyable and addictive as I do!

Cath Kidston

Stitch! Basics

The next few pages cover all you need to know about needlepoint and cross stitch, from advice on materials and equipment to detailed, illustrated instructions for creating the stitches. I've added in plenty of hints and tips for successful finishing off, and some technical background information on how to make your completed needlework up into a finished project.

Needlepoint Basics

Some projects in this book are worked in cross stitch, while others are embroidered on to canvas. But what is this second technique actually known as? Is it needlepoint, canvas work, tapestry or woolwork? There are as many opinions as there are names; although the four terms are interchangeable, I'm sticking with the first one!

Needlepoint is worked with wool (or sometimes embroidery thread) on an open weave canvas. The canvas is covered by the stitches, so unlike cross stitch, the design has a solidly stitched background. It's a wonderfully versatile technique; I've used it to create a variety of accessories and homewares, from a clutch bag to a floor rug.

All you need to get started are three items of equipment: a piece of canvas, a needle and some wool. After a few practise stitches, you'll be able to work any of my designs.

CANVAS

Needlepoint canvas is woven from tightly spun and stiffened cotton. It has a square weave of vertical and horizontal – warp and weft – threads which produce a mesh-like appearance. You stitch through the spaces between these threads. It is labelled according to how many holes there are every 2.5cm. This is known as the count: the lower the number, the larger the stitches will be. Therefore, 12-count canvas is on a smaller scale than 5-count rug canvas. The 'materials' list for each project specifies the size and count of the canvas required.

You can buy canvas in pre-cut lengths or off the roll in a white or antique (unbleached) finish. The best quality canvas is unlikely to distort as you sew: check it isn't over-stiffened and the threads are not fraying.

There are three different types of canvas:
• Mono interlock canvas is used for half cross and tent stitch. The twisted mesh holds the stitches in place so they do not slide between the woven threads.

• Mono canvas is fine for straight stitch designs, like the bargello cushion and for working continental tent stitch. If you can find it, choose the 'de luxe' version.

• Duo or Penelope canvas is woven from pairs of thread, and is good for half cross stitch. In needlepoint it is used for tramming and petit point.

NEEDLES

Tapestry needles have a blunt tip so that they won't split the canvas threads or damage the previous stitches as you sew. They also have a long, wide eye to accommodate thick yarn. They come in various sizes to go with the different count canvases: the lower the number, the thicker the needle.

Buy a mixed pack and pick out a needle that goes through the canvas holes without forcing the threads apart, but that doesn't slip through too easily. A size 18 is the standard for 10-count canvas, a 20 is used for a 12- or 14-count and a finer size 22 for delicate 16-count. You might need a supersized 14 for the rug, which holds up to three lengths of wool at a time.

YARN

The wool needlepoint projects are worked with DMC tapestry yarn, a soft, single stranded 4-ply wool that is sold in 8m skeins. It is available in an inspiringly wide spectrum of colours, and the exact shades and quantities needed for each project are listed under 'materials'. (The equivalent colours from the Anchor range can be found on pages 151–5). Stranded embroidery thread is an interesting alternative to wool. Sew with all six strands at the same time and thread the needle as shown for yarn. Mount the canvas on a frame to keep the stitches regular.

CUTTING THE YARN
The skeins of wool are held together with two paper bands, the lower one wider than the other – don't be tempted to take these off as you'll soon get in a tangle. Hold the skein firmly by the narrow top band and gently pull the loose length at the bottom end.

The yarn has to pass back and forward through the canvas many times as you stitch. To prevent it becoming frayed, work with a length of around 50cm. Once you start stitching, you may find that the yarn starts to turn back on itself. If this happens, simply hold your work upside down and the needle will spin round as the yarn untwists.

THREADING THE NEEDLE
To get the end of your wool through the eye of a tapestry needle, hold it by the top end and with the other hand, fold the final 3cm of yarn over the point. Pull the yarn down to tighten and hold the resulting loop securely between your finger and thumb. Slide the needle out and push the eye down over the loop.

STARTING AND FINISHING
Now you're ready to go! As with so many aspects of needlepoint, there are several ways of starting and ending your stitches, but this is the method used by professional embroiderers and gives the neatest finish.

• WASTE KNOT
Make a knot at the end of the yarn and take the needle through the canvas, from front to back, about 2cm away from your starting point. As you work, the strand of yarn at the back will be anchored by the stitches. When it is covered, simply snip the knot close to the canvas.

• WASTE END
If you are using a frame, you can finish off in a similar way. Bring the last 6cm of yarn up within an area that has yet to be stitched, 3cm from the end of the row. Make a short stitch, leaving the tail on the right side. Unpick the stitch and trim the tail when the yarn at the back as been covered.

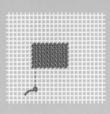

• WOVEN FINISH
Another way to finish off is to slide the needle under the back of the last 2cm of stitches. Trim the end close to the surface. This is sometimes easier if the canvas isn't mounted but it can create a slight ridge on the right side. You'll have to use this method with the last few lengths used in a design.

Basic Stitches

This is the simplest and most versatile needlepoint stitch, which is always used for charted designs. A small, slanting stitch, worked diagonally over the intersection of two canvas threads, it creates a smooth surface which resembles a woven fabric.

Just to confuse things, there are three ways of working tent stitch. They all look the same from the right side of the canvas, and all have different names! Which variation you use is really up to you, but I'll explain the different methods of construction and benefits of each one. In the instructions for the projects I usually suggest that you use half cross stitch, but you may prefer to work in tent or even basketweave – you choose!

HALF CROSS STITCH

This method is the most economical as it uses the least yarn, but this makes it marginally less hardwearing than the other two methods and produces a slightly flatter stitch. It can be sewn from side to side or up and down: on the reverse side you will see rows of short vertical or horizontal stitches. It should always be worked on interlock or duo canvas.

Bring up the needle at the top of the stitch and take it down diagonally, over one intersection to the left. Come up again one thread above, to start the next stitch and continue to the end of the row.

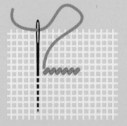

The next row is worked below or above this row, from left to right. You may find it helps to turn the canvas upside down, so you are always making stitches in the same direction.

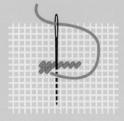

TENT OR CONTINENTAL TENT STITCH

My favourite method. It's very quick to work without a frame, as you can push the needle in and out in a single scooping action for each stitch. It can also be worked in horizontal or vertical rows of plump stitches. On the back of the canvas it appears as a line of longer sloping stitches, and because it uses more wool, it gives a thicker finish. You can use mono, interlock or duo canvas.

Work the first row from right to left. Start at the bottom of the first stitch and take the needle up diagonally to the right, over one intersection. Bring the point out to the left, behind two intersections, and through the next hole. Carry on to the end of the row.

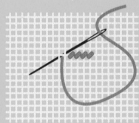

The next row is worked above or below the first in the opposite direction, from left to right. Again, try turning the canvas the other way up, so that the direction of the stitches remains constant.

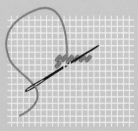

BASKETWEAVE TENT STITCH

This is worked diagonally, on either mono or duo, as it doesn't distort the canvas very much. It is often recommended for backgrounds and, because it has a padded reverse side, was traditionally used for seat covers. The back lives up to its name, having a dense interwoven appearance. It takes about twice as much thread as half cross stitch.

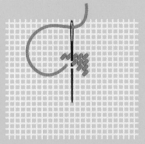

Starting at the top right corner, work the first two stitches vertically as for continental tent stitch. Make the third stitch next to the first, and the fourth next to the third.

Advanced Stitches

Most of the needlepoint in this book, especially the more detailed designs based on my fabric prints, is worked entirely in tent stitch, which creates an almost pixillated image. There are, however, many other needlepoint stitches which will add texture and detail: here are the ones that I have used.

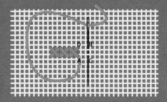

CROSS STITCH

To give them a raised appearance, needlepoint cross stitches are sewn singly, rather than in two stages. Work over two intersections for 12- or 10-count canvas, but over a single intersection with double yarn for 5-count rug canvas.

Make a slanting upwards stitch from A to B then a second one from C to D. Repeat to the end of the row.

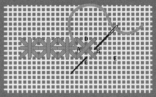

DOUBLE CROSS STITCH

This stitch is also known, rather poetically, as Leviathan stitch or Smyrna cross. It's made by stitching an upright cross over a single cross stitch. It's worked over four thread intersections.

Make a single cross stitch, then work a horizontal stitch from A to B and a vertical stitch from C to D. Start the next double cross at E, then continue in the same way.

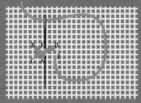

LONG ARMED CROSS STITCH

This border stitch consists of a row of overlapping asymmetrical crosses which produce a solid, plait-like outline. It's worked over two horizontal and four vertical intersections.

Start the row with a diagonal stitch from A to B. The first cross is worked from C to D and then E to F. Come out again at A ready for the next cross.

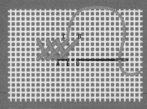

PLAIT STITCH

A wider version of long armed cross, work this stitch over two, three or four horizontal intersections, depending on the required width.

The first cross is made from A up to B and the second from C down to D. Start the next cross at E, and repeat along the row.

SLOPING GOBELIN STITCH

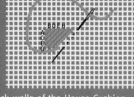

This is a versatile stitch that can be worked over two, three or four intersections. I used blocks of it for the brick walls of the House Cushion and vertical lines for the roofs, reversing the direction of the slant on alternate rows.

Depending on the depth of the row, start with one, two or three upwards slanting stitches in the top left corner, worked from A to B, C to D and E to F. G to H is the first full stitch – repeat this to the end of the row and fill in the triangular space with shorter stitches.

CUSHION STITCH AND CUSHION VARIATION STITCH

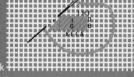

These little squares are made up of five graduated diagonal stitches. You can work them all in the same direction or alternate the slant on every other row to vary the effect. Both methods were used for the two Spot Cushions on page 42.

The first square is worked from A to B, C to D, E to F, G to H and I to J. Continue working from right to left, starting the next square at K. The rows of stitches can also be worked from vertically, but the squares must always line up.

MOSAIC STITCH

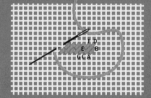

A smaller variation of cushion stitch, this is a versatile filling, which I used for the Electric Flower Cushion on page 62 and the Spot Doorstop on page 118. Mosaic stitch can also be worked vertically and you can vary the direction of the slant if you wish.

Work the first square from A to B, C to D and E to F. Start the next square at G and carry on stitching from right to left.

FLORENCE STITCH

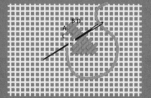

Made up of diagonal rows of alternate long and short stitches, this useful filling adds an interesting texture.

Start the first row at top left with two diagonal stitches from A to B and C to D. Repeat these as many times as necessary, working downwards. The next row is worked upwards, so that the long and short stitches interlock. Vary the length of the stitches to fill the space.

FRENCH KNOTS

I couldn't resist using these little round knots in the window boxes of the House Cushions on page 58, although they are not usually found in needlepoint. Practise a few to get the hang of the technique first.

Wrap the yarn twice around your needle to make two loops. Keeping the yarn taut, push the point down through the canvas, one thread away from the hole where it emerged.

Cross Stitch Basics

Cross stitch is simple and versatile, easy to learn and because you work on to a fabric with a grid-like weave, all your stitches will be perfectly regular, right from the start. To bring a fresh approach to a favourite craft, I went through all my designs in search of those that would translate well into cross stitch. I particularly like the bright sail boat motif and interpreted it on two different scales. The tiny sprigged Lavender Heart and Spot Tea Cosy are perfect projects for beginners (both quick to work) but for a longer commitment choose the endearing House Picture. The great thing is that the basic technique is just the same for all four.

FABRIC

Most of the projects are worked on specially designed, slightly stiffened cross-stitch fabric, also known as Aida cloth. It has a block weave, which gives the surface a pattern of woven squares with holes at the corners. Each stitch is worked over a single block. The closer together the holes, the finer the stitches will be and the more detailed the design. Like canvas, cross-stitch fabric is graded by the number of holes per 2.5cm. I used a larger scale 8-count fabric for the Sail Boat Beach Bag, a medium 11-count for the Bouquet Knitting Bag and a finer 14-count cloth for the Lavender Hearts. It comes in a white, ecru and range of pastel and brighter colours.

SOLUBLE CANVAS

This is a wonderful innovation which allows you to stitch cross-stitch designs on to garments, fine lawn, or denim – in fact, any fabric that doesn't have an even weave. It looks like a fine transparent plastic and is punched with a series of small holes that lie in a grid pattern, equivalent to 14-count cloth. Cut out a piece slightly larger than your finished design and tack it securely to the background fabric. Embroider your design as usual, then wash the finished project to dissolve the canvas. Do make sure fabric is pre-shrunk before you start to stitch, just in case.

NEEDLES

As with needlepoint, work with a blunt tipped needle that will not damage the cloth or split the stitches. Fine tapestry needles are sometimes labelled as cross-stitch needles: pick a size 26 for 14-count fabric or a size 24 for 11-count. You can even add a touch of luxury to your work by using gold-plated needles, which glide easily through the fabric! If you are using soluble canvas you'll need an ordinary embroidery needle with a long eye and a sharp point to pierce the background fabric.

STRANDED EMBROIDERY THREAD

All the cross-stitch projects are worked in DMC stranded thread. This lustrous cotton is produced in a wonderful range of colours, and I've picked out shades that match my own distinctive palette. It comes in 8m-long skeins and consists of six finely spun strands of smooth cotton, which are loosely twisted together. These can be separated and recombined, depending on the size of stitch required. Fine 14-count designs on Aida cloth and soluble canvas use just two strands, 11-count designs use four strands and for larger-scale 8-count designs you need all six strands. In the 'materials' list for each project you will find details of the amount of thread needed and a reference for each colour. The numbers refer to the DMC range, but equivalent shades from two other manufacturers – Anchor and Madeira – are listed on pages 151–5.

Getting Started

PREPARING THE THREAD

The skeins of thread are designed to unravel easily, but make sure you pull in the right direction, or you'll get in a tangle. Hold the skein by the short band at the top and pull down on the loose end of thread from the bottom end. You will need a length of around 50cm to work with – any more and it will fray before you finish and your stitches will look untidy.

Hold the middle of the cut length gently but firmly between finger and thumb and carefully pick out the end of a single strand with the other hand. Pull the strand out of the bundle, maintaining the tension so that the other five threads don't snag up. Remove the number of individual threads you need in this way and lay them out together, side by side. Thread all of them through the needle at the same time, using the same technique as for tapestry yarn on page 15.

STARTING AND FINISHING

It may sound a bit obvious, but you should always start and end a length of thread in the correct way. Knots leave lumps and bumps on the back of the fabric, and badly finished 'tails' have a habit of working loose. Follow these methods and your work will always be smooth and even.

INVISIBLE START

When working with an even number of strands, there's an ingenious way to start off without a knot. Cut a metre length of thread and separate out one, two or three strands. Fold the strand or strands in half and thread the cut ends through your needle. Take the needle down at A, the starting position of the next half cross stitch and bring it back up in the finish position B, leaving the loop on the surface of the fabric. Slip the needle through the loop and pull the thread gently to form the first half cross stitch.

Take the needle back down through B, then carry on stitching as usual. Be careful not to pull the loop too tightly or the fabric will distort. But do make sure you are in the right place if starting this way, as it's not easy to undo!

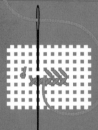

WASTE KNOT

When you are working with an odd number of strands, use a waste knot as for needlepoint. Thread the needle and knot the other end. Take the needle down from the front, about 3cm from the point where the next stitch begins, in a position where the loose thread will be trapped on the wrong side by the cross stitches. Carry on stitching towards the knot and clip it close to the surface when the thread is anchored.

FINISHING OFF

Turn the work over once you finish the last stitch. Slide the needle horizontally under the upright stitches at the back for about 2cm, then pull it through so the thread lies under the stitches. Clip the end, leaving a tuft of about 3mm. Do not pull the thread tightly or the final stitch will go out of shape.

HOW TO CROSS STITCH

Each cross stitch is made up of two diagonal half cross stitches, one worked over the other. To give a professional look to your embroidery, work them so that the second halves of the cross all lie in the same direction – it doesn't really matter which way this is, as long as they all match.

CROSS STITCH ROWS

This is the quickest way to cover large areas and is economical with thread. The reverse side appears as rows of short upright stitches. Work in horizontal rows, from right to left to right or left to right – it doesn't matter which way, as long as the second stitches of each cross all lie in the same direction to produce a smooth, regular surface. You may find it easier to work in vertical rows to fill in some parts of a design.

Start at the bottom right corner, at A and take the needle diagonally up to B to make the first half cross stitch. Repeat this to the end of the row.

Start the second row of stitches at C and take the needle down at D. Carry on stitching from left to right, until all the half stitches are covered.

SINGLE CROSS STITCHES

Come up at A and take the needle diagonally across and up to B to make the first half cross stitch. The second stitch is worked from C to D. You can work a short row in this way, starting the next cross at C and working from right to left.

DIAGONAL LINES

Each cross stitch in a diagonal line is worked individually. You may need to use this technique for letters or for angled outlines. Make the first stitch from A to B and C to D, then come out at E to start the next one. This is worked from E to F and G to C. Repeat this, making sure all the top stitches lie in the same direction.

Getting Ready To Stitch

PREPARING THE BACKGROUND

Whether you're about to embark on a needlepoint or a cross-stitch project, you'll need to prepare your background fabric before you start sewing. Aida cloth might be creased and canvas still curved from the roll, so the first thing to do is to press it well. If you are going to use soluble canvas, launder the garment or fabric it if has not yet been washed.

Although it may seem time consuming, it's worth taking time to neaten the edge of Aida cloth with a narrow hand-stitched hem or a machine zigzag, to prevent it fraying. If you are not using a frame, bind all four sides of your canvas with masking tape, otherwise the yarn will snag on the rough edges (and if you are using a frame, and are feeling virtuous, you can bind just the side edges). Do make sure that you don't use a low-tack tape however, or it will simply peel off!

MARKING THE CENTRE

Most projects begin with the instruction to mark the centre of the fabric. This gives you a guideline for positioning the stitches, which corresponds with the vertical and horizontal centre lines marked on each chart. It also helps to ensure the grain lies straight within the frame.

Fold the canvas or cloth into quarters and sew a line of running stitch over each crease. Use a bright coloured sewing thread and stitch along a single line of holes: this is easily unpicked when your work is complete.

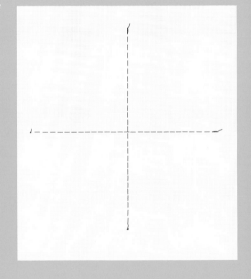

FRAMING UP

Keeping the fabric under tension within a frame helps to keep your stitches regular. This is especially true with needlepoint; some distortion is inevitable when a diagonal stitch is worked over a canvas with a square weave, and for stitches like bargello and cushion which are made over several threads of canvas. Even so, the decision whether to use a frame or not is a matter of personal preference. Sewing without one means your work is more easily portable. Like many others, I find it more relaxing to sit back in an armchair with my canvas in my lap (and something interesting on the television of course!).

SEWING WITH A FRAME

Working with a frame requires a two-handed sewing method, with one hand above the canvas to push the needle down and the other hand poised below, ready to push it back up to start the next stitch. Which hand goes where depends on whether you are left or right handed, so if you haven't sewn this way before, try some practise stitches until you find a rhythmic action that is comfortable for you.

If you have an old-fashioned floor-standing frame or a hoop on a stand that can be clamped to a table, make sure that it is set at the right level, so that you don't have to lift your arms too high, or hunch over it. Scroll and stretcher frames can be propped up against a table, across the arms of a chair or over your knees if you prefer to sit on the floor.

You should always stitch in good light. Natural daylight is ideal, but good task lighting, directed over your shoulder, is fine during the dark evenings. Just be sure not to let any shadows fall across your work and always double check the codes of each colour thread as they can look quite different by artificial light.

TYPES OF FRAMES

If you do mount your canvas, it should be in a rectangular frame to maintain the square weave of the canvas or fabric. There are two types to choose from:

STRETCHER FRAMES

These consist of two pairs of narrow wooden struts, which slot together at the corners. You can interchange the pairs to create different shaped frames. Painters use these stretcher frames to mount their canvas, and a wide range of sizes can be found at your local art supplier. The smallest frames are very useful for small-scale projects like the pencil cases.

Pick a frame that is the same size as your canvas – you can always allow a wider margin so that the canvas fits the frame exactly. Fix the centre point of each side of the canvas to the frame with drawing pins or a staple gun, pulling it slightly to create a little tension, then pin out towards the corners. If the centre markings are going out of true, simply adjust the pins to straighten up the grain of the fabric.

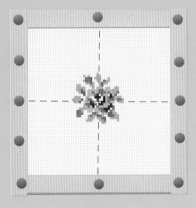

Getting Ready
To Stitch

ROLLER FRAMES

Also called scroll frames, these are made up of two lengths of dowel, along each of which is stapled a length of cotton webbing. They are held together with two short side struts, which have a v-shaped slot at each end, and are secured by screws and wing nuts. The canvas can then be rolled up as you work: if you are working a large-scale design, only part of it will be visible.

The frame should be no more than 20cm wider than your canvas. Stitch the webbing centrally to the top and bottom edges, then slot on the struts. Adjust the rollers so that the centre point of the canvas lies in the middle of the frame and then tighten the wing nuts at the top. Roll the bottom bar until the canvas is taut and secure the other two wing nuts. Lace the side edges of the canvas over the struts with strong thread so that it feels like a drum. As your stitches progress, you will need to turn the rollers and re-do the lacing so that the unworked canvas sits within the centre of the frame.

EMBROIDERY HOOPS

Cross-stitch fabric can also be mounted in a rectangular frame, but most embroiderers like to use a lighter weight wooden hoop, in which the fabric is sandwiched between two wooden rings. The inner ring is solid and the outer one open, and held in place with an adjustable screw. Hoops are available in diameters from 10cm to 40cm: find a size that will leave plenty of fabric around your stitches.

Loosen the screw to remove the outer ring. Spread the fabric centrally over the inner ring and slide the outer ring over the top. Gently pull each edge of the fabric to increase the tension. Check that the crossed stitch lines are still straight, then tighten the screw.

The only problem with a hoop is that it can leave indentations in your work. Binding the inner ring with cotton tape can help prevent this and it also stops the fabric from slipping. It's a good idea to take the fabric out of the frame each time you finish stitching. If you are working on a larger project, like the knitting bag, you may have to move the hoop so that part of it lies over completed stitches. Placing a sheet of tissue paper between the fabric and outer ring will reduce the pressure on the stitches: simply tear away the paper within the ring to reveal the area to be stitched next.

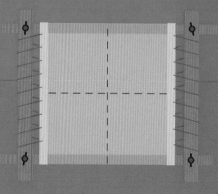

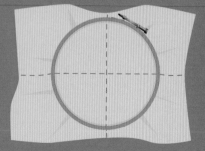

Starting To Stitch

I have given you detailed step-by-step instructions with each of the projects, showing how to stitch the individual charts, and then how to make up the finished embroidery. Whether this is simply mounting it in a frame, or turning it into a lined bag with handles, all the technical aspects are illustrated with clear diagrams.

The book has been designed for stitchers with varying levels of knowledge, from novice to expert. If you're just starting out I'd recommend one of the smaller projects – a Provence Rose Pincushion or a Motif Badge – which are quick to make and don't involve a lot of extra sewing. To help you choose, each project has been given a skill rating, from a basic 1, up to a more complicated 3. Experienced workers can always skim over some of the more basic advice.

Have fun with the designs and interpret them as you like. You may prefer to make the Union Jack Cushion design up as a straightforward picture (and it would look fabulous in a vintage frame) or embroider the Stanley Badge design directly on to a kid's denim jacket with soluble canvas. I have always thought that the Electric Flower design would make a stunning rug, worked in repeated squares, in cross stitch on 5-count canvas with double yarn!

HOW TO READ A CHART

The charts for counted cross stitch and tent stitch are the same: a pattern of coloured squares in a grid formation. Each square represents a single cross stitch worked over one block of the cross-stitch fabric or a single tent stitch worked over one thread intersection. Like graph paper, the grid is divided by heavier lines every ten squares, making it easier to count the stitches. The vertical and horizontal centre lines are marked clearly on each chart. These correspond with the two lines of tacking on the background fabric. For other needlepoint stitches and for bargello designs, the coloured squares represent part of a longer stitch. The colours and exact stitches used are fully explained in the first steps of each project.

Photocopy the particular chart that you are working from, enlarging it a little to make it easier on the eyes. As with charted knitting patterns, crossing out or blocking off the areas you have worked helps track your progress – and it gives a sense of achievement.

SHADE CARD

Alongside the chart is a key, which gives the DMC reference number of the embroidery thread or tapestry yarn for each colour. It's a good idea to make a shade card before you start a project, so you have a sample of every thread with their colour codes. Punch holes along a strip of cardboard and fix a length of yarn through each one. Write the reference number next to each shade, so if the paper bands slip off, you'll always know which colour goes where.

It's a good idea to buy all the skeins needed at the same time, especially for larger areas like the background of the cowboy cushion, as colours can vary between dye lots. No two stitchers will use the same amount of yarn or thread, so the amounts given are generous and allow for a little unpicking.

UNPICKING

We all make mistakes, but luckily misplaced or uneven needlepoint stitches are easily remedied. With the tips of your embroidery scissors or an unpicker, cut through the centre of each stitch, taking care to avoid the canvas threads. Pull the resulting tufts out from the reverse side (tweezers help if they get stuck) and use adhesive tape or a lint roller on any stray strands.

ORDER OF WORK

Start with the group of stitches that lies closest to the central crossed lines. Count carefully and make one stitch for each square. If the next area of the same colour lies less than 2.5cm away, take the thread behind the fabric and bring the needle up to start stitching. If it is further away, finish off and start again. Do not carry long 'floats' or loose stitches across the back between blocks of stitches, as they can get tangled. Remember darker threads show through the holes of cross-stitch fabric.

As a general rule, continue working up towards the top edge and then down towards the bottom edge of the design. Some charts, however, will need to be worked in another order; it's always easiest to stitch outlines first, then fill them in. The little house design is a good example of this, where you start off with the doors and windows, then add the details, whilst the bargello needlepoint designs both start at the top left corner. I've suggested a logical way of working for all of the projects, which may be helpful.

BLOCKING AND FINISHING

When you have completed your final stitch, remove your work carefully from the frame. All you need to do with cross stitch is to press it lightly from the wrong side to remove any creases, first placing it face down on a clean tea towel. Needlepoint, however, may need a little more attention. You might find that your

neat rectangular canvas has turned into a rhomboid. Don't worry... you can easily 'block' it to get rid of the distortion. The size, or stiffening agent, in the canvas threads is water soluble, so when it is damp the canvas can be pulled back into their original shape.

Make a paper template the size of the finished piece and mark the centre point of each edge. Tape it centrally to a drawing board and cover with a piece of cling film or clear plastic that is 5cm larger all round. Use a laundry spray to dampen the stitches and place the canvas face down on the cling film. Match the tacked centre lines with the midpoints of the template to square it up and place a drawing pin at each of these points, 2cm from the edge of the stitches. You may need to stretch it to make them line up exactly. Pull the four corners into position and pin down, then add more pins at 2cm intervals. Leave the board in a warm place to dry naturally, then unpin the canvas.

AFTERCARE

You will have invested hours in creating your cross-stitch or tapestry projects, so take great care of them. Fine needlework produced by previous generations is now valued as heirloom pieces. Direct sunlight causes fading, and remember that anything made from 100% wool is vulnerable to moth attacks. If the stitches get grubby, use a vacuum cleaner with a soft brush attachment or the foot of an old pair of tights taped over the nozzle, to get rid of any loose dust or grit.

Small spots can be removed with gentle soap and a moist cloth, but washing isn't advisable as it removes the stiffening and can felt the stitches. However, if you need to take drastic action and a piece is really dirty, gently rinse it in tepid water with soapflakes, then stretch out to dry naturally. Canvas should be pinned out on a board, as for blocking. Specialist dry

Sewing Essentials

When it comes to making up the needlepoint or cross-stitch pieces into a final project, many of the smaller items in this book can be stitched together by hand. You may even prefer to make up cushion covers by hand too, but a sewing machine is required for some larger items, like the Sail Boat Beach Bag. Your sewing machine doesn't need to be the latest high-tech invention, as all you need to do is a straight stitch and the occasional zigzag.

WORKBOX EQUIPMENT

In addition to the tapestry wool, stranded cotton embroidery thread and needles used for embroidery, you will need some basic needlework tools and haberdashery. For neatness, keep these bits and pieces all together in a sewing basket. Likewise, store your work-in-progress and stretcher or roller frame in an old cotton pillowcase to protect it from any damage. Stock your sewing basket with the following:

• a mixed packet of needles with a few long-eyed embroidery needles and some thicker sewing needles to start with.

• embroidery scissors, with short blades and a pointed tip are essential for cutting threads and trimming knots.

• manicure scissors are good for unpicking and snipping stray stitches.

• household scissors are useful for cutting canvas and should also be used for cutting out paper patterns – never use dressmaker's shears or scissors on paper.

• dressmaker's shears, which have long angled blades, are necessary for accurate cutting of backing and lining fabrics.

• an unpicker, specially designed to cut safely through stitches, may prove helpful from time to time.

• long dressmaker's pins with round glass heads are strong enough to go through thick fabrics and will show up well against the stitches. Keep them to hand in a pincushion – if you haven't got one, the needlepoint Provence Rose Pincushion could be your first make!

• a tape measure is essential for calculating lengths of fabric.

• sewing threads should match the colour of the backing fabric or the predominant colour in the needlepoint. Number 50 mercerized cotton is a good all-purpose thread for natural fibres that will stitch through canvas and thicker fabrics. Pick a contrasting colour for tacking so that the stitches stand out.

Sewing Essentials

FABRICS

Selecting the right trims and fabrics is a vital part of making up your projects: it's exciting when you come across the perfect velvet, linen or silk to back a cushion or line a bag. Sometimes I'll choose a material that perfectly co-ordinates with the threads, like the pink linen on the Spot Doorstop, but I also like unexpected colour combinations that clash.

Search for backing fabrics that are similar in weight to the canvas or Aida cloth, such as antique linen, vintage upholstery fabric, velvet and my own cotton duck prints. Lining fabrics can be lighter, so hunt down suitable dressmaking or haberdashery cottons and silks. Although the inside of a bag isn't always visible, I love hidden details like the golden satin I used for the Spray Clutch Bag lining.

CUTTING OUT

The materials list for each project includes the size of fabric required for backing and lining panels. One-off shapes like the Lavender Heart are given as template, but for squares and rectangles you can make your own paper patterns.

Do this by drawing the given measurements out on a sheet of squared dressmaker's paper and cutting out along the grid lines. Pin the pieces to the right side of the fabric, so one edge lies parallel to the grain, then cut around the edge with shears.

CUSHION PADS

Ready-made pads, with feather or polyester fillings, come in a range of sizes. Not all of my cushion designs are standard shapes, however, so you may have to make your own pad. Don't feel daunted by this as it's actually very straightforward.

Cut two pieces of calico or cotton ticking, each 2cm larger all round than the given cushion pad size. Wirh right sides facing, pin together the two pieces around the outside edge, then machine stitch with a 2cm seam. Leave a 10cm gap along one side. Clip a triangle from each corner, cutting diagonally 5mm from the seam. Press back the seam allowance, including that along both sides of the opening. Turn the cushion case right side out through the gap. Stuff the case with polyester cushion filler, a loose fibre available from any good furnishing suppliers. Pin the two sides of the opening and sew by hand or machine to close.

Finishing Touches

It's the details that give individuality to any piece of needlework, so I always like to spend time carefully planning my projects... and sometimes changing my mind along the way! I knew that the handles for the Bouquet Knitting Bag were just right when I first saw them, but the Bargello Cushion on page 34 was originally edged with a vintage red braid. Later on I came across the jolly bobble fringing and knew that it was a much better alternative... so the woollen braid had to go. Don't ever be afraid to swap things round in the search for the perfect finishing touch!

PASSEMENTERIE

This evocative French word is defined as 'ornamental decoration or adornment' and encompasses the range of furnishing or dressmaking trims, from fringing to piping and braids.

• Fringing works well with needlepoint. You'll find many extravagant versions, but sometimes a simple cotton fringe, like the one I used on page 38 is all you need. I customised this to suit the Spot Cushions: as it was too long, so I trimmed it back to 1cm for a fresher look.

• Bobble fringing has an irresistible, light-hearted appeal. As with piping, it can be stitched into a cushion cover as it's put together, but it's much easier to add afterwards, by hand. Position it so that the woven edging lies on the back panel then stitch along the top and bottom edges.

• Piping, a loosely twisted cotton cord covered with a narrow bias strip of fabric, creates a coloured outline that defines a seam visually around the edge of a cushion or padded case.

To make your own piping, you must make your own bias binding. First, cut fabric strips on the bias (with the grain of the fabric running diagonally). Trim the ends of each strip diagonally, at 45 degrees. To join two strips, pin together with the right sides facing and the ends overlapping as shown. Seam between the points where they cross.

Press the seams open and trim off the projecting triangles. Fold the strip in half lengthways, with wrong sides together and press. Press each edge in turn towards the centre fold.

Finishing Touches

To complete the piping, take a narrow bias binding strip and fold it around a length of twisted cotton piping cord with the wrong sides facing. Tack close to the cord and unpick any visible tacking once the seam is completed.

Piping is stitched in place between the front and back panels, either by hand or machine. This is an advanced technique but you can achieve a similar result by hand-stitching narrow cord along a finished seam. To finish, make a tiny slit in the seam, close to the corner, and push the ends of the cord through the gap and secure them with a few stab stitches.

• Ricrac is a narrow braid that is woven in a continuous wavy line. I trimmed the Sail Boat Candleshade on page 000 with this, stitching it behind the lower hem so only a little line of scallops is visible.

• Lace is too delicate to go on needlepoint, but if you can find any heavier edgings, they work well with cross stitch. I used a simple broderie anglaise for the Lavender Heart on page 000 and a vintage guipure for the Provence Rose Pillow. Sew by hand with small, unobtrusive stitches.

• Pompons always look bright and perky, so I couldn't resist adding one to the top of the Spot Tea Cosy on page 128 (where you will also find making-up instructions.) You can alter the size of the pompon by varying the diameter of the cardboard foundation discs.

FINISHING OFF

The edging for your cushion or case should always be finished neatly. There is a special technique for overlapping the ends of piping, shown in detail within the relevant projects, and sometimes loose ends can simply be concealed at a corner.

If you've used lace or a frilled edging you will have to join two cut ends, so allow an extra 2cm for the turnings. At the start, fold the first 5mm to the wrong side then stitch the bottom edge around the cushion. When you've gone all the way round, trim the surplus back to 1.5cm. Turn back the final 5mm so that it lies towards the front before you stitch it down. Overlap the neatened ends by 1cm and sew the two layers together along the folds and the top edge.

Stitch! Projects

Editing and selecting the projects for this book was a nigh-on
impossible task as there were so many possibilities! In the end,
I tried to choose as wide a range of techniques and ideas as possible,
including a pincushion to make in an afternoon and a rug that could
take a year. Whatever your skill set I hope you find inspiration and
enjoyment in all the designs I finally chose.

Bargello Cushion

MATERIALS

• 40cm square 12-count mono canvas tapestry frame • DMC tapestry wool in the following colours: white (blanc); yellow (7049); red (7106); pink (7202); green (7386); fawn (7411); blue (7802) – 2 skeins each • tapestry needle • 34cm square floral print backing fabric • dressmaker's pins • sewing machine • sewing needle • matching sewing thread • 140cm length braid or fringing • 30cm square cushion pad

The flowing waves of this traditional Bargello design are built up from blocks of vertical stitches of various lengths, worked in horizontal rows. The technique dates back to Renaissance Italy, but I've given my cushion a contemporary twist with a bright new colour palette and an unexpected flowery backing.

1 The vertical stitches mean the canvas will not distort, as tends to happen with diagonal stitches. If you prefer to work without a frame, simply bind the edges of the canvas with masking tape. Mark the starting point for the first row of stitches 7cm diagonally in from the top left corner.

2 Thread your needle with green yarn and bring it up through the canvas at the starting point. Following the Bargello Cushion chart, on which each vertical block of coloured squares represents one straight stitch worked over six horizontal canvas threads, work the first row of green stitches.

3 The next row is worked in yellow and interlocks with the first. Start three threads down from the first green stitch: bring your needle up here and insert it at the base of the first stitch. Continue the row, working all the stitches in the same direction.

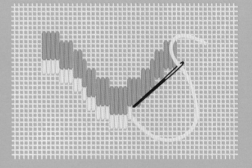

4 Continue the design for the cushion front, changing colours and altering stitch lengths as indicated on the Bargello Cushion chart. Fill in the gaps at the upper and lower edges to give a perfect square.

5 Once the design is complete, press lightly from the wrong side. Trim the excess canvas down to a 2cm margin all round.

top tip TO MAINTAIN AN EVEN TENSION BARGELLO STITCHES MUST BE WORKED IN THE SAME DIRECTION – FROM BOTTOM TO TOP.

Bargello
Cushion

6 With right sides facing, place the cushion front on top of the backing panel. Pin and tack the two together all round the outside edges. With the cushion front uppermost, sew along the line where the unstitched canvas and the stitching meet. Leave a 20cm opening along the lower edge.

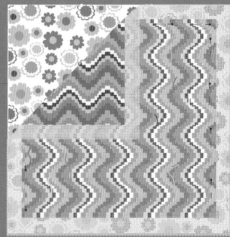

7 Clip a triangle from each corner – cut diagonally 5mm from the corner – then trim another narrow triangle from each side. Press back the seam allowances either side of the opening.

8 Turn the cushion cover right side out. Using the blunt end of a pencil, carefully ease the corners out into neat right angles.

9 Insert the cushion pad and pin together the two sides of the opening. Using a double length of thread, slip stitch the edges together by hand to close the gap.

10 Using small slip stitches and matching sewing thread, sew the braid to the cushion. Line up the bottom edge of the braid along the seam line as you sew. Gather the braid slightly at each of the corners and finish off the ends as described on page 34.

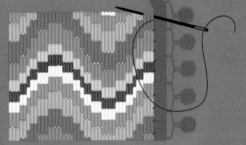

top tip A WELL-CHOSEN EDGING FINISHES OFF A CUSHION IN THE SAME WAY THAT A GOOD FRAME ENHANCES A PAINTING.

I CHOSE THIS PERKY BLUE POMPON TRIM BECAUSE IT COMPLEMENTS THE COLOURS OF BOTH FRONT AND BACK.

Spot
Cushion

MATERIALS

For the blue cushion • 40cm square 10-count canvas • tapestry frame • DMC tapestry wool in the following colours: off-white (7510) – 2 skeins; blue (7555) – 16 skeins • 36cm square natural linen backing fabric • 130cm length cotton fringing • 30cm square cushion pad

For the red cushion • 30cm square 10-count canvas • DMC tapestry wools in the following colours: red (7106) – 7 skeins; off-white (7510) – 1 skein • 26cm square natural linen backing fabric • 90cm length cotton fringing • 20cm square cushion pad

For both • tapestry needle • scissors • dressmaker's pins • sewing needle • matching sewing thread

SKILL LEVEL: 1

So far my versatile spot design has popped up on everything from a baby buggy and a bath mat to wall-paper and clogs. I couldn't resist finding just one more use for it – this time on two blue and red square needlepoint cushions. They work together well as a pair or piled on a sofa, alongside a row of floral print cushions.

1 Start both cushions in exactly the same way, following the Spot Cushion chart. The outer square gives the size of the larger blue cushion; use the inner outline for the smaller red cushion. Working outwards from the centre of the canvas, stitch the spots in half cross stitch (see page 16) using the off-white yarn.

2 The blue background is worked in cushion stitch (see page 19). Start the first row at the top left corner, with a square block of five diagonal stitches. Continue along to the right corner, then stitch the following rows directly

below, all in the same direction. You will need to make shorter diagonal stitches to fit around the spots.

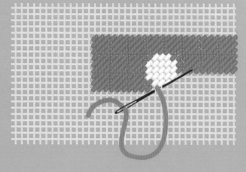

3 The red background is worked in cushion variation stitch (see also page 19). You may find it easier to reverse the canvas, by holding it the opposite way up, when you are working the left-sloping stitches.

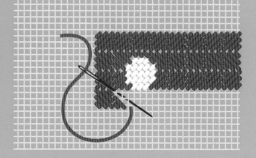

---

top tip CUSHION STITCH IS WORKED DIAGONALLY, WHICH DISTORTS THE CANVAS, SO THE BLUE CUSHION MAY NEED TO BE BLOCKED. THE RED ONE USES CUSHION VARIATION STITCH, SO AS THE ROWS SLANT IN ALTERNATE DIRECTIONS IT WILL NOT NEED STRAIGHTENING OUT.

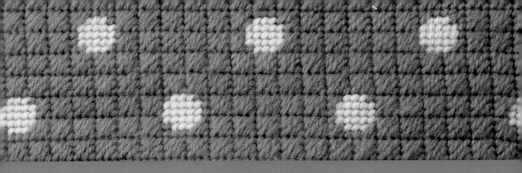

4 Make up both cushions in exactly the same way. Once the design is complete, press lightly from the wrong side. Trim the excess canvas down to a 2cm margin all round. Place the cushion front right side down on a folded tea towel and press back 5mm of stitching at each corner at a 45 degree angle. Press back the edges to give a squared-off mitre at each corner.

5 Press back and then unfold a 3cm turning along each edge of the backing panel. Press across the corners, squaring them off as before, then re-press the creases along all four edges. The backing panel should now be the same size as the front.

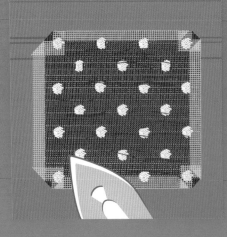

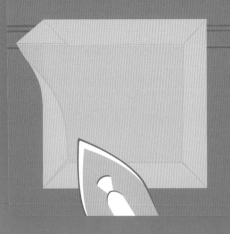

Bargello Cushion

6 Starting at one corner, pin and tack the fringing to the wrong side of the backing panel, so the fringe lies beyond the neatened edge. Fold the woven part of the fringing at a 45 degree angle at the next three corners, and overlap the ends when you have completed the round. Cut off the loose end.

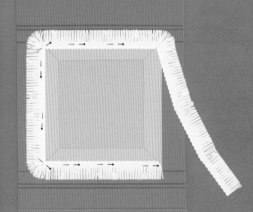

7 With wrong sides facing, pin the cushion front to the backing panel around three sides, so that the fringing is sandwiched between the two. Slip stitch these three sides together, passing the needle through the fringe. Insert the cushion pad, then pin, tack and stitch the fourth sides together.

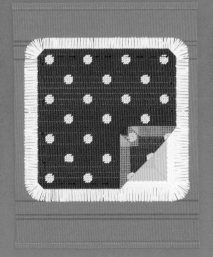

top tip IF YOU CAN'T FIND THE PERFECT EDGING, DON'T FORGET THAT YOU CAN ALWAYS CUSTOMISE. THIS FURNISHING FRINGE COMPLEMENTED THE CUSHIONS PERFECTLY, BUT IT WAS A BIT TOO LONG... SO I SIMPLY TRIMMED IT DOWN WITH MY SHARPEST SCISSORS!

Provence
Rose Pillow

MATERIALS

• 20 x 50cm 11-count cross-stitch fabric in white • DMC stranded cotton embroidery thread in the following colours: mid-green (562); light pink (963); coral (3705); light coral (3706); light cream (3865) – 1 skein each; light green (564) – 2 skeins; light blue (747) – 3 skeins • small tapestry needle • 50 x 90cm blue fabric • 24 x 40cm cushion pad (see how to make this on page 32) • 90cm length lace edging • dressmaker's pins • sewing machine • sewing needle • matching sewing thread

CUTTING OUT

from the blue fabric cut • one 26 x 44cm front panel • two 26 x 28cm back panels

SKILL LEVEL: 1

The little needlepoint pincushion on page 100 worked so well that I wanted to see how the rose motif looked as a repeat design... and I'm very pleased with the result. Re-coloured in shades of coral and jade green it makes an elegant cross-stitch centre panel for this narrow boudoir cushion.

1 Mark the centre of the cross-stitch fabric. Bind the edges of the fabric with masking tape or mount it in a tapestry frame if you wish. The design is worked in cross stitch throughout using four strands of the embroidery thread. Following the Provence Rose Pillow chart, and starting in the centre of the fabric, work the first motif. Stitch the rose, then the leaves and the buds.

2 To make sure you get the correct distance between each rose, start the next two motifs by working the leaves nearest to the centre rose, leaving one unstitched square between

them. Work a further three motifs on each side of the first rose.

3 Next, work the pale blue decorative border along both the upper and lower edges, repeating it as many times as necessary to match the number of rose motifs.

4 Once the design is complete, press lightly from the wrong side. Trim the excess cross-stitch fabric back to a 3cm margin along the long edges and a 2cm margin along the short edges. Place the cross-stitch panel right side down on a folded tea towel and press back the top and bottom turnings.

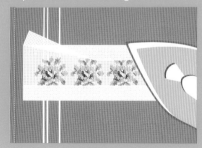

top tip   YOU COULD ALSO USE THIS DESIGN AS AN EDGING FOR A FLUFFY WHITE TOWEL, ON A FABRIC BAG OR EVEN AROUND A LARGE DRUM-SHAPED LAMPSHADE.

Provence
Rose Pillow

5 Cut the length of lace edging in half. Slip stitch the two pieces along the upper and lower edges of the cross-stitch panel. Start the repeat pattern at the same place on both edges so it is symmetrical.

6 Place the lace-edged fabric panel centrally across the cushion front. Pin along the upper and lower edges.

7 Using matching sewing thread, machine stitch the lace-edged fabric panel down. Sew carefully and slowly between the first two rows of cross stitches.

8 Press back a 1cm turning along one short edge of a backing panel, then fold it back once more and press again to make a double hem. Machine stitch the hem down, 5mm from the edge. Hem the second backing panel in exactly the same way.

9 With right sides facing and raw edges matching, pin one backing panel to the cushion front so the hemmed edge lies across the centre. Pin the second backing panel to the other side of the front, overlapping the hemmed edges.

10 Machine stitch all round the edge of the cushion, leaving a 2cm seam allowance. Trim the seam allowance back to 1cm and clip a small triangle from each corner to reduce the bulk. Turn the cushion cover right side out and insert the pad.

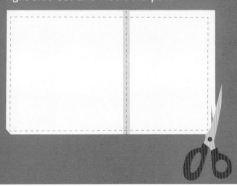

top tip I FILLED IN THE LIGHT CREAM DOTS WITHIN THE BLUE BORDERS, BUT YOU COULD TRY LEAVING THESE UNSTITCHED TO CREATE A MORE LACE-LIKE FEEL.

Union Jack Cushion

MATERIALS

• 30 x 40cm 10-count canvas • tapestry frame • DMC tapestry wool in the following colours: dark red (7108); yellow (7455) – 1 skein each; mid-pink (7223); beige (7230); green (7391) – 2 skeins each; grey-blue (7705) – 3 skeins; dark pink (7758) – 8 skeins • tapestry needle • 50cm square lightweight denim fabric • 110cm length 6mm piping cord • two 24 x 22cm rectangles striped ticking backing fabric • 20 x 30cm cushion pad (see how to make this on page 32) • dressmaker's pins • sewing machine • matching sewing thread

SKILL LEVEL: 3

The design for the Union Jack pencil case on page 82 was such fun to do that I decided to develop it further, by continuing the floral sprig pattern to form a border around the central flag. A selection of more subdued shades gives the resulting cushion a softer vintage appearance, which is completed by the faded look of the denim piping.

1 Mark the centre of the canvas. Bind the edges of the canvas with masking tape or mount it in a tapestry frame. The design is worked in tent stitch throughout. Following the Union Jack Cushion chart, work in the order given on page 82.

2 Once the central flag is complete, stitch the additional sprigs within the outer border and fill in the dark pink background. Once the whole design is complete, remove the canvas from the frame and block if necessary. Trim the excess canvas down to a 2cm margin all round.

3 Make a bias strip from the denim fabric to cover the piping cord. Draw a line at a 45 degree angle from the bottom left corner up to the right edge. Mark two more parallel lines above this, each 4cm apart. Cut along these lines.

4 With light blue sides facing, overlap the ends of the two denim strips at right angles and pin together. Machine stitch, leaving a 6mm seam allowance, then trim the spare triangles of denim at each end. Press the seam open and cut the strip down to 105cm. Press back a 1cm turning at one end.

top tip IF, LIKE ME, YOU ARE USING A TICKING TO MAKE THE BACKING, MAKE SURE THAT THE STRIPES RUN ALONG THE
LENGTH OF BOTH PIECES. THEY WILL THEN APPEAR UPRIGHT ON THE FINISHED CUSHION.

Union Jack Cushion

5 Fold the denim strip lengthways over the piping cord leaving a 'tail' of 2cm. Starting 3cm from the end, tack the two sides of the fabric together, leaving the final 3cm unstitched.

7 Fold the neatened end of the denim strip over the raw end when they meet. Trim the piping cord so that the ends butt and stitch them loosely together. Fold the uppermost end of the piping back over and tack down.

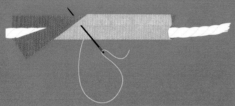

6 Starting at the centre of the lower edge of the needlepoint, tack the piping all round the cushion front. Position it so that the cord lies inwards and the tacking stitches run along the edge of the woollen stitches. Make a small cut into the denim at each corner so that the piping bends round at right angles.

8 Hem the backing panels following the instructions given in step 8 on page 49. With right sides facing and raw edges matching, pin and tack one backing panel to the cushion front so the hemmed edge lies across the centre. Pin and tack the second panel to the other side, overlapping the hemmed edges.

9 Fit a zipper foot to your sewing machine so the stitches lie alongside the piping cord. With the cushion front uppermost, sew all round along the line where the unstitched canvas and stitching meet. Clip a triangle from each corner to reduce the bulk. Press the seam allowances at front and back inwards.

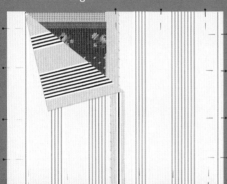

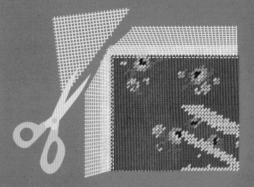

10 Turn the cushion cover right side out, carefully ease the corners out into neat right angles, and insert the pad.

top tip THE 20 X 30CM PAD USED TO FILL THE CUSHION IS NOT A STANDARD SIZE THAT YOU CAN BUY READYMADE, BUT YOU CAN FIND OUT HOW EASY IT IS TO MAKE YOUR OWN ON PAGE 32.

Spray Flower Cushion

MATERIALS

• 30 x 45cm 11-count cross-stitch fabric in ecru • DMC stranded cotton embroidery thread in the following colours: light green (772); ecru (842); mid-pink (899); green (992); dark pink (3350); turquoise (3766) – 2 skeins each; light pink (604); light gold (676); brown (3857) – 1 skein each • fine tapestry needle • 100cm length frilled edging • 22 x 34cm linen backing fabric • 18 x 30cm cushion pad (see how to make this on page 32) • dressmaker's pins • sewing machine • sewing needle • matching sewing thread

SKILL LEVEL: 2

Here is one of my very favourite floral spray designs, this time making an appearance as a cross-stitch motif. I've re-interpreted it in bright summery shades of embroidery thread to make a luxurious boudoir cushion – the perfect gift for a best friend, sister, mother or aunt (providing you can bear to part with it).

1 Mark the centre of the cross-stitch fabric. Bind the edges of the fabric with masking tape or mount it in a tapestry frame if you wish. The design is worked in cross stitch throughout using all six strands of the embroidery thread. Following the Spray Flower Cushion chart, and starting in the centre of the fabric, work the large pink roses, then the smaller blue flowers, the leaves and finally the dots.

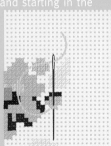

2 Once the cross-stitch design is complete, press lightly from the wrong side. Trim the excess fabric down to a rectangle measuring 22cm high x 34cm wide. To ensure the design remains central, measure a point 4cm from the first stitch on each side. Cut along the rows of holes in the fabric that line up with these points.

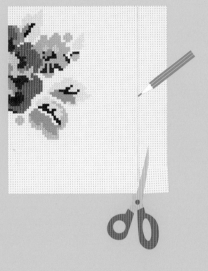

top tip THE STITCHES ARE WORKED WITH SIX STRANDS OF THREAD TO CREATE A DENSE TEXTURE. IF YOU WISH TO MOUNT THE FABRIC, USE A RECTANGULAR FRAME OR A LARGE HOOP WITH A CIRCUMFERENCE OF 35CM OR MORE, SO THAT THE STITCHES WILL NOT GET DAMAGED.

Spray Flower
Cushion

3 With right sides facing, place the backing panel on top of the cushion front. Pin and tack the two pieces together all round the outside edges.

4 With the cushion front uppermost, machine stitch all round the edge of the cushion, leaving a 2cm seam allowance. Leave a 15cm opening along the lower edge. Sew a few extra diagonal stitches across each corner so that they will be slightly rounded.

5 Clip a small triangle from each corner – cut diagonally 6mm from the corner stitches – then trim another narrow triangle from each side. Press back the seam allowances all round the cushion cover, including on either side of the opening along the lower edge.

6 Turn the cushion cover right side out. Using the blunt end of a pencil, carefully ease the corners out into neat rounded curves.

7 Insert the cushion pad. Pin and tack together the two sides of the opening. Slip stitch the edges together by hand to close the gap.

8 Fold over 1cm at one end of the frilled edging, then fold it once more to conceal the raw end. Stitch down the folded end. When adding the edging to the cushion cover, ensure that this folded end lies on the wrong side of the cushion.

9 Sew the frilled edging to the cushion by hand with matching sewing thread. Starting at the centre of the lower edge, use small slip stitches along the seam line. Gather the edging slightly at each corner.

10 When the edging has been added to all four sides and you are back at the starting point, trim the loose unstitched end to 2cm and neaten as in step 8. Stitch the two neatened ends of the edging securely together.

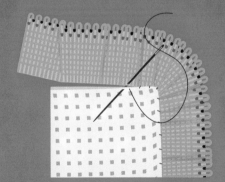

top tip THE FILLING PAD IS STITCHED INSIDE THE CUSHION COVER TO GIVE A NEAT FINISH TO THE BACK. IF YOU NEED TO DRY
CLEAN THE COVER AT ANY TIME, ALL YOU HAVE TO DO IS UNPICK THE STITCHES ALONG THE OPENING AND TAKE OUT THE PAD.

House
Cushions

MATERIALS

• three 40cm squares 10-count canvas • tapestry frame • DMC tapestry wool in the following colours: ecru; yellow (7472) – 4 skeins each pink (7004); dark blue (7306); mid-green (7386); red (7666) – 3 skeins each; pinky-red (7106) – 7 skeins; dark cream (7141) – 10 skeins; dark green (7541) – 6 skeins; dark red (7544) – 1 skein; brown (7622) – 8 skeins; light green (7771); mid-blue (7802) – 2 skeins each • tapestry needle • 210cm length bobble fringing • 30 x 80cm red check backing fabric • 60 x 80cm calico • polyester cushion filling • sewing machine • matching sewing thread

House Cushions

SKILL LEVEL: 3

This bolster – a highly desirable terrace of three cottages – is a long-term project that will keep you occupied for weeks. Like the striped rug, it is also a sampler, which introduces some of the textured needlepoint stitches featured on pages 17–19. Have fun with this design. Either copy my choice of stitches or improvise with your own.

1 All three sections of the cushion are worked in exactly the same way. However, when stitching the second and third canvases, remember to work the roofs in either red or mid-green and the doors in either pink or light green. Mark the centre of one piece canvas. Bind the edges of the canvas with masking tape or mount it in a tapestry frame if you wish. The design is worked in a combination of needlepoint stitches (see pages 17–19). Following the House Cushions chart, and starting in the centre of the canvas, work the door's outline and portico, handle, studs and letterbox in half cross stitch. Add the brown steps in mosaic or slanting gobelin stitch. Fill in the blue door with mosaic stitch, the other steps and path in slanting gobelin stitch and the porticos in mosaic or Florence stitch.

2 Next, work the window outlines in half cross stitch and the sills in a single row of cushion stitch. Fill in the panes, curtains and flowers in half cross stitch with a few French knots, if you wish, to add texture to the petals.

3 Work the berries in half cross stitch and the bushes around them in half cross or Florence stitch. Stitch the brown gutter in mosaic or tent stitch. Fill in the blue roof in slanting gobelin stitch and the sky in Florence stitch. (The blue house has sky only on the right; the green house has it only on the left.)

4 Finally, fill in the wall with 'bricks' of eight slanting gobelin stitches worked over four canvas threads. Adjust the length of the diagonal stitches to fit around the other features and change the direction of each row.

5 Once the design is complete, remove the canvas from the frame and block if necessary. Trim each canvas down to a 2cm margin all round. With right sides facing pin the houses together in the right order, matching the edges of the needlepoint. Machine stitch along the edges of the stitching. Press the seams open.

6 Using the completed canvas as a template, cut out the backing panel and two pieces of calico for the cushion pad. Make up the cushion pad as described on page 32.

7 With right sides facing, pin the 'terrace' to the backing panel. Machine stitch all round the edge of the cushion front, leaving one short end unstitched. Press the seam allowances inwards. Turn the cushion cover right side out. Insert the pad and pin together the two sides of the opening. Using a double length of thread, slip stitch the edges together by hand to close the opening. Hand sew the fringing all round the edge, neatening the edges as described on page 34.

top tip IF YOUR TIME (AND MAYBE YOUR PATIENCE) ARE LIMITED YOU COULD MAKE UP THE CANVASES ONE AT A TIME AND TURN THEM INTO THREE DETACHED HOUSES.

Electric Flower Cushion

MATERIALS

- 45cm square 10-count canvas • tapestry frame • DMC tapestry wool in the following colours: mid-pink (7135) – 4 skeins; dark pink (7136) – 6 skeins; dark blue (7287) – 2 skeins; green (7406) – 2 skeins; yellow (7470) – 2 skeins; off-white (7510) – 5 skeins; light blue (7594) – 1 skein • tapestry needle • 130cm fine piping
- 34cm square dark pink backing fabric • 30cm square cushion pad • sewing machine with zipper foot
- sewing needle • matching sewing thread

SKILL LEVEL: 2

My boldly graphic electric flowers design is the perfect showcase for introducing some new needlepoint stitches. The background and outlines are all worked in half cross stitch but the petals and flower centres are filled in with diagonal mosaic and Florence stitches, which gives them extra depth and texture.

1 Bind the edges of the canvas with masking tape or mount it in a tapestry frame if you wish. Mark the starting point for the first row of stitches 10cm diagonally in from the top left corner.

2 The design is worked in a combination of half cross, mosaic and Florence stitch and involves a lot of detailed counting.

Following the Electric Flower Cushion chart, work the outline of the top left flower in half cross stitch. Fill in the centre and the petals with mosaic stitch.

3 Contine to work the rest of the design, stitching the flower outlines first and then filling the centres and petals in with either mosaic or Florence stitch. The Electric Flower Cushion chart is annotated to show exactly where each stitch is used. The smaller flowers are all worked in half cross stitch.

4 Once the flowers are complete, fill in the dark red background using half cross stitch.

5 Once the whole design is complete, remove the canvas from the frame and block if necessary. Trim the excess canvas down to a 2cm margin all round.

top tip STITCHING INSET PIPING CAN PROVE A LITTLE FIDDLY, SO YOU MAY PREFER TO HAND STITCH A CORD OR OTHER NARROW TRIMMING AROUND THE FINISHED CUSHION.

6 Starting at the centre of the lower edge, tack the piping all round the cushion front. Position it so that the join between the cord and braid runs along the edge of the woollen stitches. Overlap the ends of the piping and make a small cut into the braid at each corner so that the piping bends round at right angles.

7 With right sides facing, place the backing panel on top of the cushion front. Pin and tack the two pieces together all round the outside edges.

8 Fit a zipper foot to your sewing machine so the stitches lie alongside the piping cord. With the cushion front uppermost, sew all round along the line where the unstitched canvas and stitching meet. Leave a 20cm opening along the lower edge. Clip a triangle from each corner to reduce the bulk, then press back the seam allowances either side of the opening.

9 Turn the cushion cover right side out. Using the blunt end of a pencil, carefully ease the corners out into neat right angles.

10 Insert the pad and pin together the two sides of the opening. Using a double length of thread, slip stitch the edges together by hand to close the opening, passing the needle through the piping from front to back, just below the cord.

 top tip ADD TO THE VIBRANT APPEARANCE OF THIS CUSHION BY USING A LUXURIOUS BACKING FABRIC:

I SOURCED A RICH VELVET TO MATCH THE DARK PINK YARN.

Bargello
Hippie Bag

MATERIALS

• 42 x 46cm 12-count mono canvas • tapestry frame • DMC tapestry wool in the following colours: light blue (7294); off-white (7331); brown (7515) – 2 skeins each; orange (7303) – 5 skeins; dark blue (7336) – 3 skeins; yellow (7485); green (7541) – 4 skeins each • 10 assorted skeins DMC tapestry wool or 80m knitting wool for strap • tapestry needle • 36 x 40cm floral print backing fabric • 36 x 80cm lining fabric • sewing machine • sewing needle • matching sewing thread

SKILL LEVEL: 1

From the Woodstock generation to Glastonbury, this fab needlepoint bag will appeal to flower children of all ages. Its unstructured shape gives plenty of room for knitting, shopping or even files and books. But why not just leave your work behind, sling it over your shoulder, and head off for a summer festival!

1 Bind the edges of the canvas with masking tape or mount it in a tapestry frame. Mark the starting point for the first row of stitches 8cm diagonally in from the top left corner.

2 Thread your needle with orange yarn and bring it up at the starting point. Following the Bargello Hippie Bag chart, on which

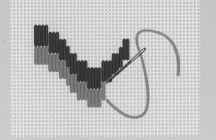

each vertical block of coloured squares represents one straight stitch worked over six horizontal canvas threads, work the first row of orange stitches. The next interlocking row is worked in yellow, with each stitch worked over five threads.

3 Continue the design for the bag front, changing colours and altering stitch lengths as indicated on the Bargello Hippie Bag chart. To finish, fill in the gaps at the upper and lower edges to give a perfect rectangle.

4 Once the design is complete, press lightly from the wrong side. Trim the excess canvas down to a 2cm margin all round.

5 With right sides facing, place the bag front on top of the backing panel. Pin and tack the two pieces together along both side and bottom edges. With the bag front uppermost, carefully machine stitch along the line where the unstitched canvas and the stitching meet.

top tip TO ADD A HANDY INSIDE POCKET, PRESS A 1CM TURNING AROUND THREE SIDES OF A 20CM SQUARE OF LINING FABRIC. MAKE A DOUBLE HEM ALONG THE FOURTH SIDE. SEW TO THE LINING BEFORE YOU MAKE IT UP, SO THE HEM LIES 10CM IN FROM ONE SHORT END.

Bargello Hippie Bag

6 Clip a triangle from both bottom corners – cut diagonally 5mm from the corner – to reduce bulk. Press back the seam allowances at front and back. Press under a 2cm turning around the bag's opening. Turn the bag right side out. Using the blunt end of a pencil, carefully ease the corners out. Press lightly.

7 Fold the lining in half and pin the side edges together. Machine stitch with a 2cm seam allowance, then press the seam allowances inwards. Press under a 4cm turning around the lining's opening.

8 Slip the lining inside the outer bag, matching up the side seams. Pin the top edges together, ensuring that both the lining and the outer bag are on exactly the same level.

9 Overstitch the outer bag to the lining with a double length of matching sewing thread: pass the sewing needle between two woollen stitches and under the top thread of the canvas, and then through the top edge of the lining.

top tip FOR THE PLAITED STRAP, I RECYCLED LEFT-OVER YARNS FROM THIS AND OTHER PROJECTS, BUT USE ANY SPARE WOOL.

10 Cut 350cm lengths of yarn for the strap. Knot them 20cm from one end and secure the knot over a hook. Divide the threads into three groups of eight and plait them together – untwist the loose ends as you go, to avoid getting into a tangle. When the plait is 150cm long, knot the other ends together and trim both ends into a 6cm tassel.

11 Stitch one knot securely to a bottom corner of the bag and sew the plait along the seam line at the side, using a double length of sewing thread. Stitch all the way up one side of the plait, then back down the other for security. Sew the other end of the plait to the opposite side in the same way.

Spray
Clutch bag

MATERIALS

• 30 x 45cm 10-count canvas • tapestry frame • DMC tapestry wool in the following colours: mid-pink (7195) –
2 skeins; light pink (7221); dark blue (7296); light green (7376); dark green (7396); dark cream (7411);
dark brown (7432); gold (7494); dark pink (7758) – 1 skein each; teal green (7927) – 4 skeins • tapestry needle
• gold lining fabric: 22 x 34cm for the flap and 34 x 40cm for the bag • iron-on wadding: 19 x 29cm for the
flap and 29 x 34cm for the bag • dark blue velvet: two 22 x 34cm rectangles for the bag • dressmaker's pins
• sewing machine • matching sewing thread • sewing needle

SKILL LEVEL: 3

The muted colours of this floral clutch will add a touch of traditional elegance to any evening outfit. The sumptuous roses are stitched in warm coral tones on a teal background, and the softly padded bag is made from blue velvet, lined in an old gold silk to tone with the yarns used for the smaller flowers and leaves.

1 Mark the centre of the canvas. Bind the edges of the canvas with masking tape, or mount it in a frame if you wish. The design is worked in half cross stitch throughout. If you prefer use tent stitch, but remember to allow 30% extra yarn.

2 Following the Spray Clutch Bag chart, and starting in the centre of the canvas, work the large pink roses. Continue to work the design

outwards with the smaller blue and gold flowers, green and gold leaves and spots. Finally, fill in the background with teal green.

3 When the design is complete, remove the canvas from the frame and block if necessary. Trim the excess canvas down to a 2cm margin all round. Press the canvas back along the side and bottom edges, then unfold the creases. Press the bottom corners inwards at 45 degrees. Clip a triangle at each corner, refold to mitre and re-press.

4 Position the iron-on wadding for the flap, adhesive side down, across the back of the needlepoint. Tuck the edges under the pressed-back canvas at the side and lower edges. Iron it in place, following the manufacturer's instructions.

top tip TAKE A TIP FROM PROFESSIONAL DRESSMAKERS: NEVER PRESS VELVET FROM RIGHT SIDE, OR YOU WILL FLATTEN THE PILE.
LAY A TOWEL OVER YOUR IRONING BOARD AND PLACE THE VELVET RIGHT (PLUSH) SIDE DOWN BEFORE STEAM PRESSING LIGHTLY FROM THE BACK.

Spray
Clutch Bag

5 Press a 2cm turning along the side and lower edges of the flap lining and mitre the corners. With wrong sides facing, pin the lining to the side and lower edges of the flap. Overstitch these edges together with matching sewing thread. Tack the unstitched lining to the canvas, 1.5cm from the top edge.

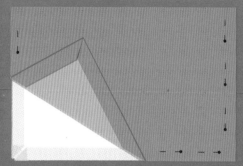

6 Pin the bag pieces together along the side and lower edges, with the plush sides facing. Machine stitch with a 2cm seam allowance, then press the seam allowances inwards. Clip a triangle from each bottom corner. Turn the bag right side out and lightly press. Pin and tack a 1.5cm turning around the opening.

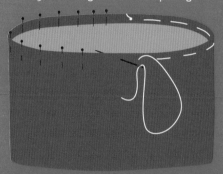

7 Fold the bag lining in half lengthways. Pin the sides and stitch with a 2cm seam allowance. Press the seam allowances inwards, then press back a 2cm turning around the opening.

8 Fold the lining wadding around the lining. Tuck the top edges under the turning at front and back, and pin in place. Press gently to fuse the two together.

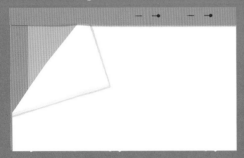

9 Slip the lining inside the bag, so that the top edge lies 5mm below the edge of the bag. Pin and tack the two together along the front edge.

10 Slot the top edge of the flap into the back of the bag, between the velvet and lining. Pin it in place, so that the row of tacking stitches lies 5mm below the folded top edges of the bag and lining.

11 Slip stitch the top edge of the lining to the flap, passing the needle through the canvas to hold it in place, but not through the velvet. Working from the other side, slip stitch the folded edge of the bag to the canvas, following a row of stitches to maintain a straight line.

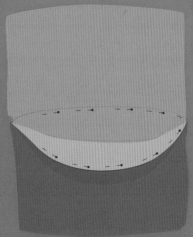

top tip USE PLENTY OF PINS AND SHORT TACKING STITCHES TO HOLD THE FRONT AND BACK OF THE BAG TOGETHER WHEN YOU ARE STITCHING THE SIDES, TO PREVENT THE TWO PIECES OF VELVET 'CREEPING' OUT OF ALIGNMENT WHEN YOU STITCH.

Sail Boat
Beach bag

MATERIALS

• 30 x 35cm 8-count cross-stitch fabric in ecru • DMC stranded cotton embroidery thread in the following colours: dark red (498); red (817); blue-green (926); dark blue-green (930) – 1 skein each • tapestry needle • 21 x 25cm medium weight iron-on interfacing • 100cm length 1cm-wide braid • 100cm x 140cm ticking fabric • 50 x 130cm spot lining fabric • 100cm length 3cm-wide braid • matching sewing thread • sewing machine

CUTTING OUT

cut each piece so stripes are centred and run top to bottom **front and back:** two 40 x 50cm rectangles **sides:** two 12 x 40cm strips **base:** one 12 x 50cm strip **lining:** one 40 x 117cm rectangle, plus one 12 x 50cm strip

SKILL LEVEL: 3

Here's a roomy bag with a seafaring air, that's big enough to carry everything that you need for a day on the beach. The pocket is made from 8-count cross-stitch fabric, which is satisfyingly quick to stitch. It gives the embroidery a solid look, which complements the striped ticking and spotty lining.

1 Mark the centre of the cross-stitch fabric. The design is worked in cross stitch throughout using all six strands of the embroidery thread. Following the Sail Boat Beach Bag chart, and starting in the centre of the fabric, work the main red sail. Continue to work the design outwards with the second sail, the masts and waves, then the clouds and gulls.

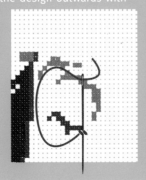

2 Once the design is complete, trim the pocket back to a 25 x 29cm rectangle, ensuring that the motif remains central. Position the iron-on interfacing, adhesive side down, on the wrong side of the stitched pocket, so that there is a 2cm margin all round. Iron the interfacing in place, following the manufacturer's instructions.

3 Press the corners of the pocket inwards at a 45 degree angle to mitre them, then press back each of the margins.

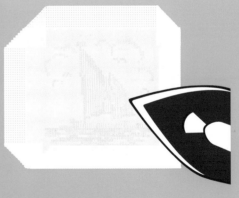

top tip I USED A RED AND WHITE TICKING FOR THE BAG BUT YOU MAY BE LUCKY ENOUGH TO COME ACROSS SOME OLD-FASHIONED STRIPED DECK CHAIR CANVAS, WHICH COMES IN TRADITIONAL SEA SIDE COLOURS.

Sail Boat
Beach Bag

4 Starting at the centre lower edge, using small slip stitches and matching sewing thread, sew the braid to the pocket. Fold the braid at an angle around each corner and finish off the ends as shown on page 34.

5 Pin the pocket centrally to the front bag panel, lining the side edges up with the stripes. Machine stitch along the side and lower edges, reinforcing both ends of the seam by working a few extra stitches in the opposite direction.

6 Now make the gusset. With right sides facing, pin one short end of each side strip to the short ends of the base. Machine stitch 1.5cm from the edge, leaving 1.5cm of fabric unstitched at each end of the seam.

7 Again with right sides together, pin one long edge of the gusset to the front panel, taking care to precisely match up the corners. Machine stitch the base, leaving 1.5cm of fabric unstitched at each end of the seam. Machine the side seams, starting from the top corners, and finishing 1.5cm from the bottom. Join the other long edge of the gusset to the back panel of the bag in the same way.

8 Turn the bag right side out. Using the blunt end of a pencil, carefully ease out the corners. Press the seams lightly, then press under a 2cm turning around the bag's opening.

9 With right sides facing, pin together the short edges of the main lining panel. Slip it inside the bag and, if necessary, adjust the width of the seam so that it fits perfectly. Machine stitch this side seam, then press the seam open. This seam lies along the centre back of the outer bag.

10 Fold the base lining panel in half lengthways to find the centre. With right sides together, pin this point to the back seam line of the main lining panel. Pin out to the corners, then pin the remaining three sides of the base panel to the lower edge of the main lining.

11 Make a 1.5cm cut into the main lining panel where it meets each corner so that the seam allowance lies flat against the

base lining panel. Machine stitch the two together, all around the base, leaving a 1.5cm seam allowance.

12 Press the seams lightly, then press under a 2cm turning around the lining's opening.

13 Slip the lining inside the bag. Pin the two together all round the opening so that the top edge of the lining sits 5mm below the top edge of the outer bag.

14 Cut the braid in half to make the bag handles. Take the first length of braid and, 15cm in from the sides, tuck 4cm at each end between the outer bag and the lining. Pin and tack the ends in place. Repeat with the second length of braid on the other side.

15 Machine stitch all round the bag's opening, 1cm down from the top edge. To reinforce the handles, sew a rectangle with a cross inside over each of the four ends of the braid.

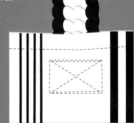

top tip IF YOU DON'T WANT TO MAKE YOUR OWN BAG, YOU COULD STITCH THE YACHT PANEL DIRECTLY ONTO A PLAIN CANVAS TOTE OR A SUMMER STRAW HOLDALL.

Bouquet Knitting Bag

MATERIALS

• 45 x 50cm 11-count cross-stitch fabric in red • DMC stranded cotton embroidery thread in the following colours: lime green (166); olive green (830); pink (956); beige (3782) – 2 skeins each; red (891) – 3 skeins; light orange (977); brown (3031); light green (3348) – 1 skein each • small tapestry needle • 45 x 150cm brown cotton fabric for the backing and lining • pair of 20cm wide knitting bag handles with slots at the lower edge dressmaker's pins • matching sewing thread • sewing machine

CUTTING OUT

• cut the brown fabric into three 40 x 45cm rectangles

SKILL LEVEL: 3

This is a really useful bag, which will easily accommodate your sewing and knitting projects, including the longest needles. It's made from red fabric and stitched with flamboyant cabbage roses. The design is reminiscent of Victorian Berlin work, but with a vivid new scheme – inspired by the rug in my hallway!

1 To find the starting point for the design, fold the cross-stitch fabric in half widthways. Now measure a point 20cm up from the bottom edge: this corresponds to the centre of the chart.

2 The design is worked in cross stitch throughout using four strands of the embroidery thread. Following the Bouquet Knitting Bag chart, and starting at the marked point on the fabric, work the large

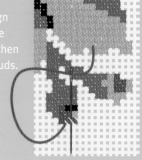

roses. Continue to work the design outwards with the smaller blooms, then the leaves and buds.

3 Once the design is complete, lightly from the wrong side to protect the stitches. Trim the fabric down to a rectangle measuring 45cm high x 40cm wide. With right sides facing, place the backing panel on top of the bag front. Pin and tack the two together along the side and lower edges. Measure 15cm down from the top on each side edge and mark with a pin.

top tip IF YOU ARE NOT A KNITTER, YOU MAY PREFER TO MAKE THIS DESIGN UP AS A FABULOUS SQUARE CUSHION OR AS A FRAMED PICTURE.

Bouquet
Knitting Bag

4 Machine stitch with a 2cm seam allowance from the marked point, leaving 15cm unstitched. Clip a triangle from the corners and press the corners inwards to mitre. Press back the seam allowances along the side and lower edges, including the unstitched parts. Press back a 2cm turning along the opening.

5 Turn the bag right side out and lightly press the seams.

6 Join the two remaining brown fabric rectangles in exactly the same way to make the lining, leaving 15cm at the top of the side seams unstitched. Press back the seam allowances as for the bag.

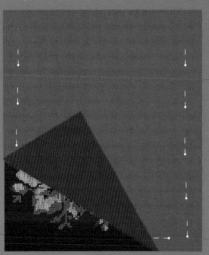
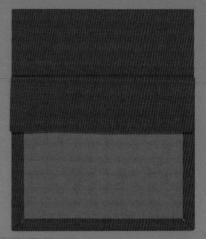

7 Slip the lining inside the bag. Pin the unstitched side edges of the bag to the lining. Starting 3cm down from the corners, oversew them together.

8 Now comes the tricky bit – fitting the bag onto the handles! Push one corner of the lining up, from back to front, through the slot at the bottom edge of one handle. Pin it to the corresponding front corner. Continue pushing the lining through the gap, pinning it to the bag front as you go. Oversew the two edges together along the folds. Sew the other handle to the back of the bag in the same way.

9 To keep the handle in position, work a row of small running stitches to join the bag and lining together, 3cm down from the top edge. Do this at the front and back of the bag.

top tip THESE HANDLES ARE MADE FROM TORTOISESHELL-LOOK PLASTIC, BUT IF YOU CAN'T FIND ANY SIMILAR, A PAIR OF NATURAL BAMBOO HANDLES WOULD LOOK JUST AS GOOD.

Union Jack
Purse

MATERIALS

• 20 x 30cm 10-count canvas • tapestry frame • DMC tapestry wool in the following colours: yellow (7504)
– 1 skein; off-white (7510) – 2 skeins; dark pink (7603) – 1 skein; light pink (7605) – 1 skein; red (7666)
– 3 skeins; blue (7802) – 2 skeins; green (7911) – 1 skein • tapestry needle • 16 x 23cm floral print backing
fabric • 20cm red zip • 23 x 30cm spot print lining fabric • sewing machine • matching sewing thread
• sewing needle

SKILL LEVEL: 3

Here's my new take on an iconic and perennially fashionable design – a Union Jack purse, embellished with tiny floral sprigs and a dusting of polka dots. A flowered backing and a lining of blue spots continue the red, white and blue theme. Don't be put off by the zip – it's really very easy to sew it in by hand.

1 Mark the centre of the canvas. Bind the edges of the canvas with masking tape or mount it in a frame. The design is worked in tent stitch throughout and involves a lot of detailed counting. Following the Union Jack Purse chart, work the white borders to the central red cross.

2 It's always easiest to work the detailed areas first, then fill in the background around them. Work the six floral sprigs inside the central cross, then fill in the red background.

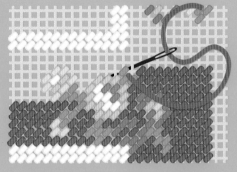

3 Next, work the red diagonals and flowers, then the white borders. Finish off by working the blue spotty triangles.

Union Jack Purse

4 Once the design is complete, block the canvas if necessary. Trim the excess canvas back to a 2cm margin all round. With right sides facing, place the purse front on top of the backing panel and pin along the side and lower edges. With the purse front uppermost, sew all round these three edges along the line where the unstitched canvas and stitching meet.

5 Clip a small triangle from each corner to reduce the bulk. Turn the purse right side out. Press under a 2cm turning around the top edge, then press the purse very lightly using a cloth to protect the surface of the stitches.

6 Fold the lining panel in half lengthways. Pin and machine stitch the side seams, leaving a 2cm seam allowance. Trim the seam allowance back to 6mm and press back. Press under a 2cm turning all round the top edge.

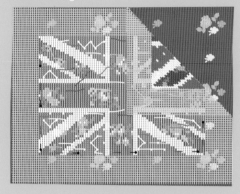

7 Open the zip fully so the pull lies at the closed end. Pin the right edge of the zip to the front of the purse, lining it up so that 6mm projects above the top edge and the teeth begin 1cm in from the corner. Tuck the other end of the zip into the purse, then pin the left edge of the zip to the back of the purse in the same way. Tack, then slip stitch in place using matching sewing thread.

8 Slip the prepared lining inside the purse. Line up the side seams, then pin the opening of the lining in place so it lies 6mm below the top edge of the zip. Slip stitch the folded edge of the lining to the zip with matching sewing thread.

top tip IF YOU DON'T WISH TO MACHINE STITCH THE PURSE, SIMPLY PRESS BACK THE CANVAS MARGIN AND THE SEAM ALLOWANCE

ON THE BACKING. HAND SEW THE TWO TOGETHER ALONG THE SIDE AND BOTTOM EDGES WITH A DOUBLE LENGTH OF MATCHING SEWING THREAD.

Stanley
Pencil Case

MATERIALS

• 35 x 25cm 10-count canvas • tapestry frame • DMC tapestry wool in the following colours: beige (7520); tan (7525); black (7624) – 1 skein each; grey (7626); red (7666) – 3 skeins each • tapestry needle
• 50cm length 3mm piping cord • 40 x 60cm grey flannel fabric for lining and piping • 16 x 25cm red cotton backing fabric • 25cm zip • sewing machine • sewing needle • matching sewing thread

SKILL LEVEL: 3

Stanley, my adorable but occasionally mischievous Lakeland terrier, has become a star in his own right. His distinctive portrait now appears on a sparkling crystal brooch and as a kidswear logo, and he even has his own fabric. For fellow fans, here's a trio of Stanleys striding across a zip-up pencil case.

1 Mark the centre of the canvas. Bind the edges of the canvas with masking tape or mount it in a frame if you wish.

2 The main part of the design is worked in tent stitch. Following the Stanley Pencil Case chart on which each coloured square represents one tent stitch, work the central Stanley. Next, add his tan and black companion to the left and then his beige and tan friend to the right. Fill in the grey background with tent stitch.

3 The red border is worked in mosaic stitch (see page 19). Following the same Stanley Pencil Case chart on which four red squares represents one mosaic stitch, work the first red mosaic stitch at the top left corner, in line with the grey tent stitch, and then continue the row towards the right. The red border is four mosaic stitches deep.

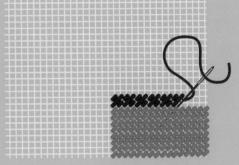

4 Once the design is complete, block the canvas if necessary. Trim the excess canvas down to a 2cm margin all round.

top tip WORKING WITH CANVAS, BACKING FABRIC AND A LINING, PLUS THE PIPING AND A ZIP CAN PROVE A BIT FIDDLY, SO I RECOMMEND STITCHING THE PENCIL CASE BY HAND TO ENSURE A NEAT FINISH.

Stanley Pencil Case

5 Press under, then unfold, a 2cm turning all round the backing panel. Mitre the corners to reduce the bulk by pressing the corners inwards, lining up the creases. Trim the tips from each of the corner triangles, and then re-press the creases. Press and mitre the corners of the stitched case front in exactly the same way.

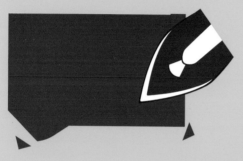

6 Prepare a 48cm length of grey piping. Follow the instructions given for covering piping cord in steps 3 to 5 of the Union Jack Cushion on pages 51 and 52.

7 Starting at one top corner of the case front, tack the piping along the side and lower edges. Position it so that the cord projects just beyond the pressed edges. Tuck the two loose ends behind the canvas, 6mm down from the top corners and trim. Make a small cut into the grey fabric at each corner so that the piping bends round at right angles.

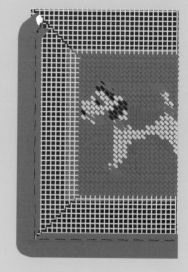

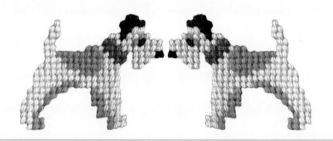

8 With wrong sides facing, place the backing panel on top of the piped case front. Pin and tack along the side and lower edges. Slip stitch the folded edges to the piping by hand. Do the same on the front for a secure finish.

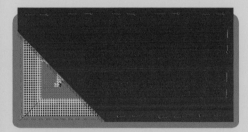

9 Open the zip fully so the pull lies at the closed end. Pin the left edge of the zip to the front of the case, lining up the tape so it sits just below the canvas. Tuck the ends into the case, then pin the right edge of the zip to the back in the same way. Tack, then slip stitch in place using matching sewing thread.

10 To make the lining cut two rectangles measuring 16cm high x 23cm wide from the remaining grey fabric. Pin and tack the two together along the side and lower edges. Machine stitch with a 6mm seam allowance. Press the seam allowance inwards. Press under a 3cm turning all round the top edge.

11 Slip the prepared lining inside the pencil case. Pin in place, matching the side seams and with the folded edge 6mm below the zip teeth. Slip stitch in place using matching sewing thread.

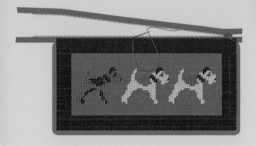

top tip THE 'INVISIBLE' ZIP IS DESIGNED SO THE TEETH LIE BEHIND THE TAPE AND CANNOT BE SEEN WHEN USED IN DRESSMAKING.

IT LOOKS ESPECIALLY EFFECTIVE HERE AS THE DISCREET FINISH MATCHES THE PIPED EDGES, BUT AN ORDINARY ZIP WORKS JUST AS WELL.

Stripe
Gadget Case

MATERIALS

• 20 x 25cm 14-count canvas • masking tape • DMC stranded cotton embroidery thread in the following colours: beige (822); light green (927) – 2 skeins each; light blue (164); dark blue (3768); coral (893); lemon (677); pink (3326) – 1 skein each • fine tapestry needle • 15 x 18cm lightweight iron-on wadding • 15 x 18cm floral print backing fabric • 18 x 24cm light blue lining fabric • dressmaker's pins • sewing machine • sewing needle • matching sewing thread

SKILL LEVEL: 1

Functional accessories don't always have to be utilitarian, as this sophisticated case proves. It's embroidered in tent stitch using six strands of thread, which gives a smooth, lustrous finish, and is backed with floral cotton. If you prefer a less pastel look, try using the colour scheme I picked for the Stripe Rug on pages 116–17.

1 Bind the edges of the canvas with masking tape or mount in a small tapestry frame if you wish. Mark the starting point for the first row of stitches 7cm diagonally in from the top right corner.

2 The design is worked in tent stitch throughout using all six strands of the embroidery thread. Following the Stripe Gadget Case chart, work each row of coloured stripes in turn.

3 Once the design is complete, remove the canvas from the frame and block if necessary. Trim the excess canvas down to a 1cm margin all round.

4 Position the iron-on wadding on the wrong side of the floral backing panel, adhesive side down. Iron it in place, following the manufacturer's instructions. Trim it down to the same size as the case front, adding a slight curve at each bottom corner.

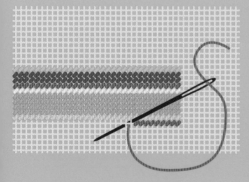

top tip THE BAG WAS DESIGNED TO FIT MY OWN SMARTPHONE. TO ADAPT THE SIZE FOR A LONGER OR NARROWER PHONE, OR YOUR MP3 PLAYER, SIMPLY INCREASE THE NUMBER OF STITCHES IN EACH ROW, OR REDUCE THE NUMBER OF ROWS YOU WORK.

Stripe
Gadget Case

5 Place the case front right side down on a clean folded tea towel and press back the margin around the side and lower edges. Press back a 2cm turning along the top edge. Fold back the bottom corners and press into gentle curves.

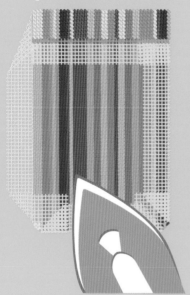

6 Press back a 1cm turning around the side and lower edges of the backing panel and then a 2cm turning along the top edge. Use only the tip of your iron to press back the edges of the fabric; try to avoid ironing the wadding – or it will go flat! Tack the turnings down all round the backing panel, easing the fabric around the gently curved corners.

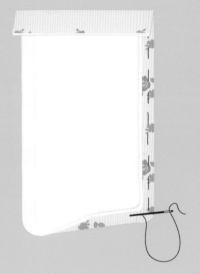

7 With wrong sides facing, place the backing panel on top of the case front and pin along the side and lower edges. Using a double length of matching sewing thread, neatly oversew these three sides together.

8 Press the lining panel in half lengthways. Trim it down to the correct size; the folded fabric should be exactly 2cm wider and 3cm deeper than the sewn case.

9 Machine stitch the side edges together, leaving a 2cm seam allowance. Press the resulting tube flat, so that the seam lies centrally on the uppermost side, then press the seam open.

10 Cut a small curve from each bottom corner, then machine stitch 1cm from the lower edge. Trim the seam allowance back to 4mm so the lining will fit neatly inside the case.

11 Press back a 1.5cm turning around the opening of the lining and tack it down.

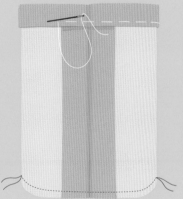

12 Slip the prepared lining inside the case. With the seam at the centre back, pin and tack the lining in place. Oversew the edges of the lining and the case using a double length of matching sewing thread.

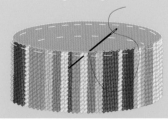

top tip YOUR PHONE SHOULD FIT SNUGLY INSIDE THE PADDED BAG, BUT FOR EXTRA SECURITY YOU CAN STITCH A BUTTON TO

THE CENTRE FRONT, CLOSE TO THE OPENING AND INSERT A FASTENING LOOP OF FINE CORD OR ELASTIC INTO THE SEAM AT THE CENTRE BACK.

Electric Flower Specs Case

MATERIALS

• 20 x 30cm 14-count mono canvas • DMC stranded cotton embroidery thread in the following colours: red (349); green (469); yellow (733); pink (3805) – 1 skein each; purple (915); lilac (3835) – 2 skeins each; off-white (648) – 3 skeins • small tapestry needle • 11.5 x 20.5cm green backing fabric • 50cm square pink cotton lining fabric • 90cm length fine piping cord • 17 x 16cm iron-on lightweight wadding • dressmaker's pins • sewing machine • matching sewing thread • sewing needle

SKILL LEVEL: 3

There will be no more excuses for mislaid reading glasses if you keep them safe in this slip-in case. It's a return appearance for the Electric Flower print, this time re-worked in bright jewel colours. Like the Stripe Gadget Case, it's stitched on fine canvas with stranded embroidery thread to produce a silky, brocade-like surface.

1 Mark the centre of the canvas. Bind the edges of the canvas with masking tape or mount it in a tapestry frame if you wish. The design is worked in tent stitch throughout using all six strands of the embroidery thread. Following the Electric Flower Specs Case chart, work the outlines of each flower, then add the coloured petals and centres and finally fill in the lilac background.

2 Once the design is complete, block the finished canvas if necessary. Trim the excess canvas back to a 2cm margin all round. Clip a small triangle from each corner – cut diagonally 5mm from the stitches. Press each corner in at a 45 degree angle, then press back the margin along each edge.

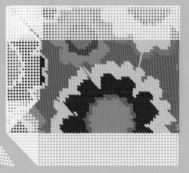

3 Prepare a 65cm length of pink piping. Follow the instructions given for covering piping cord in steps 3 to 5 of the Union Jack Cushion on pages 51 and 52.

top tip TO MAKE A CASE TO FIT YOUR COOLEST SUNGLASSES, INCREASE THE WIDTH BY ADAPTING THE COLOURS USED FOR THE CUSHION CHART ON PAGE 60.

Electric Flower Specs Case

4 Starting at the left bottom corner, slip stitch the piping around the edge of the case front. Work from the right side and position it so that the cord lies snugly against the edge of the stitching. Make a small cut into the pink fabric at each corner so that the piping bends round at right angles. Tuck both ends under the corner where they meet.

6 Prepare a 10cm length of pink piping. Tack the piping along one short edge of the backing panel. Turn back the ends of the piping at an angle and stitch them down.

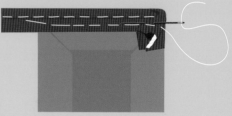

7 Working from the right side, slip stitch the piping to folded edge of the backing panel.

5 Press under, then unfold, a 2cm turning all round the green backing panel. Mitre the corners in exactly the same way as the case front. Check that the case front and the backing panel are the same size; adjust the turnings if necessary.

top tip THE PROPORTIONS OF THIS CASE COULD ALSO BE ADAPTED TO MAKE A FLORAL VERSION OF THE STRIPE GADGET CASE ON PAGE 90.

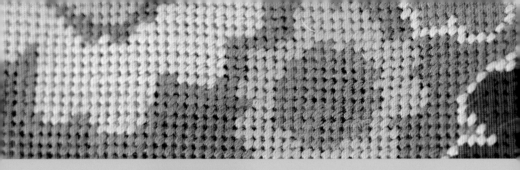

8 With right sides together, pin the backing to the front along the side and lower edges. Hand sew them together securely using a stabbing action, passing the needle from front to back just below the piping cord.

9 Cut a 17 x 18cm rectangle from the remaining pink fabric. Iron the wadding to the wrong side, matching the lower edges. Press back a 2cm turning along the top edge to cover the wadding.

10 Machine stitch the side edges together, leaving an 8mm seam allowance. Trim the seam allowance back to 5mm. Press the resulting tube flat, so that the seam lies centrally on the uppermost side, then

press the seam open. Machine stitch the lower edge, leaving a 1cm seam allowance, then trim the seam allowance back to 5mm so the lining will fit neatly inside the case. Press back a 1.5cm turning around the opening of the lining and tack it down.

11 Slip the prepared lining inside the case, with the seam at the centre back. Using a ruler or a chunky knitting needle, push the corners of the lining right down inside the case. Pin and tack the case and the lining together around the opening so that the lining lies just below the piping cord, then stab stitch together.

Motif
Badges

MATERIALS

- three 10cm squares 12-count canvas • masking tape • DMC stranded cotton embroidery thread in the following colours: light pink (151); light green (503); turquoise (598); yellow (676); mid-brown (841); dark beige (3033); dark pink (3731); red (3801); mid-green (3848); brown (3857); off-white (3865)
- tapestry needle • iron • glue stick • sewing needle • canvas bag • thimble

SKILL LEVEL: 1

Embroidering a cushion cover is rewarding but it can take many hours. For the times when you'd prefer a more instant result I came up this fun set of three badges featuring Stanley, a posy of flowers and two luscious cherries. Stitch them in an afternoon to update a canvas bag, denim jacket or even a cushion!

1 Mark the centre of the canvas. Bind the edges of the canvas with masking tape. The designs are worked in tent stitch throughout using all six strands of the embroidery thread. Following the Motif Badges charts, work the central motif, next fill in the background, then finally sew the coloured border.

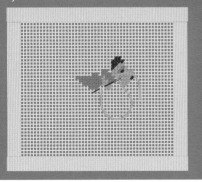

2 Once the design is complete, trim the canvas back to a 1cm margin all round.

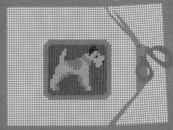

3 Place the badge right side down on a clean folded tea towel. Press the corners inwards at a 45 degree angle with the tip of a warm iron. Press the sides of the canvas inwards, folding each one carefully along the edge of the stitching. The corners are now neatly mitred. Keep the turnings in place with a slick of glue.

4 Coat the back of the badge with a thin layer of glue, then position it on your bag. Using two strands of embroidery thread in the same colour as the badge's border, slip stitch the edges to secure it in place. You will need a thimble to protect your finger tip as you push the sewing needle through the thick canvas fabric.

top tip THESE LITTLE BADGES MAKE GREAT PRESENTS FOR FRIENDS AND FAMILY SO MAKE SURE YOU HAVE SOME SPARE CANVAS.

YOU CAN STITCH ALL THREE FROM ELEVEN SKEINS OF THREAD, AND THERE WILL BE PLENTY LEFT OVER FOR A SECOND AND EVEN A THIRD SET.

Provence Rose Pincushion

MATERIALS

• 15 x 20cm 10-count canvas • DMC tapestry wool in of the following colours: white (blanc) – 2 skeins; light green (7369) – 1 skein; dark green (7386) – 1 skein; light pink (7605) – 1 skein; red (7666) – 1 skein; light blue (7802) – 1 skein; mid-pink (7804) – 1 skein • tapestry needle • 10.5 x 13cm velvet for backing • small amount of polyester wadding • sewing needle • matching sewing thread

SKILL LEVEL: 1

One of the pleasures of needlework is collecting and making the various bits of equipment that you will need for your future creations. A well-stocked workbox should always hold a needle book, a tape measure, a pair of embroidery scissors, a selection of coloured sewing threads, and – very importantly – a well-stuffed pincushion.

1 Mark the centre of the canvas. Bind the edges of the canvas with masking tape. The design is worked in either half cross or tent stitch throughout. Following the Provence Rose Pincushion chart, work the central rose. Add the leaves and buds, then work the blue border at the top and bottom. Fill in the white background, not forgetting the dots within the blue border.

2 When the design is complete, block the finished canvas if necessary. Trim the excess canvas down to a 2cm margin all round.

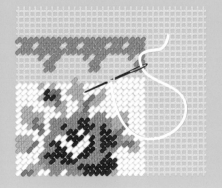

top tip THIS PROJECT IS TOO SMALL TO MOUNT IN A FRAME, SO SIMPLY BIND THE EDGES OF THE CANVAS WITH MASKING TAPE BEFORE YOU START WORK.

Provence Rose
Pincushion

3 Place the pincushion front right side down on a clean folded tea towel. Press the corners inwards at a 45 degree angle with the tip of a warm iron. Press the sides of the canvas inwards, folding each one carefully along the edge of the stitching. The corners are now neatly mitred.

4 Press back a 2cm turning along each edge of the backing panel. Check the size against the pincushion front – they should be exactly the same size, so adjust the turnings if not. Open them out again and press the four corners inwards, lining up the creases. Re-press the turnings and tack them down.

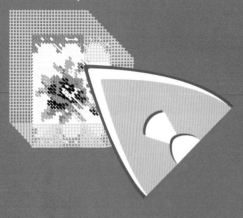

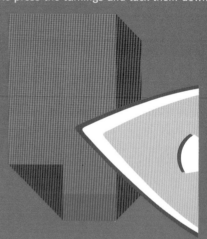

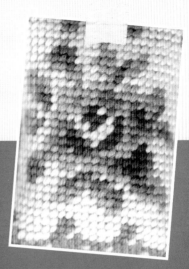

5 Hold the pincushion front and back together, with wrong sides facing. The two layers of fabric will be too thick to pin, so tack them close to the outside edges.

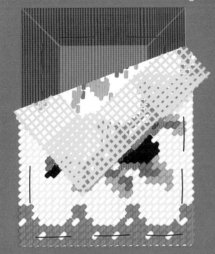

6 Sew the pincushion front to the back by hand. Make small overstitches, picking up one thread of canvas and a small amount of velvet each time. Leave a 4cm opening along one long edge.

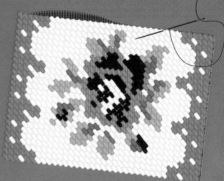

7 Stuff the cushion with the polyester wadding. Pack it down into the corners using the top of a pencil until it is really firm, then oversew the opening to close.

top tip ADD A SPOONFUL OF DRIED LAVENDER FLOWERS TO THE POLYESTER WADDING: THEIR FRAGRANCE WILL
BE RELEASED EACH TIME YOU INSERT A PIN.

Little Bunch Dungarees

MATERIALS

• pair of denim dungarees • 7cm square of soluble canvas • DMC stranded cotton embroidery thread –
1 skein in each of the following colours: blue (322); dark pink (602); light pink (819); brown (840);
green (912); red (3801) • long-eyed embroidery needle • tacking thread

SKILL LEVEL: 1

Dungarees are immensely practical for all small children, but little girls may appreciate some extra embellishment! Soluble canvas enables you to embroider cross-stitch patterns directly onto fabrics like denim, which do not have an even weave, so adding this posy to the pocket is an easily accomplished task.

1 Carefully unpick any labels or badges from the dungaree pocket. Tack the soluble canvas in place, positioning it centrally, 1cm down from the top edge. Work a couple of vertical stitches to indicate the centre of the canvas.

2 To save complicated counting, work the motif from the top downwards. The design is worked in cross stitch throughout using three strands of embroidery thread. Following the Little Bunch Dungarees chart, start with the two small leaves, which lie to either side of the centre point and 2cm down from the top edge of the pocket. Continue with the

pink and red roses, then the blue flower, the remaining leaves and finally the stalks.

3 When the design is complete, trim away the surplus canvas. To dissolve the soluble canvas, carefully wash the dungarees in warm soapy water following the manufacturer's instructions. Rinse thoroughly, then allow to dry and iron as usual.

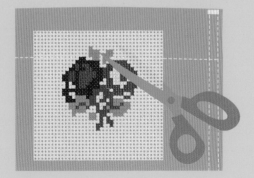

top tip YOU MIGHT FIND IT HELPS TO SLIP YOUR 'NON-SEWING' HAND INTO THE POCKET TO SUPPORT THE FABRIC
WHILST YOU ARE SEWING, AND TO WORK THE MOTIF SIDEWAYS RATHER THAN THE CORRECT WAY UP.

Sprig Border Dress

MATERIALS

• 5 x 15cm soluble canvas • DMC stranded cotton embroidery thread – 1 skein in each of the following colours: ecru (ecru); green (368); lemon (445); dark pink (892); pink (894); light blue (3753) • embroidery needle • tacking thread

SKILL LEVEL: 1

I was delighted to come across this tiny lace-trimmed petticoat in an antique market. It's hand stitched from the finest cotton lawn with a softly gathered frill at the hem. All it needed as the finishing touch – decades after it was first made – was a scattering of embroidered flowers across the yoke.

1 Fold the yoke of the dress in half to find the centre. Mark this point with a vertical tacking stitch.

2 Cut a 4 x 5cm piece of soluble canvas and tack it in place centrally on the yoke.

3 The design is worked in cross stitch throughout using two strands of embroidery thread. Following the Sprig Border Dress chart, work the pink flower of the centre motif, then the green leaves and the remaining flower details.

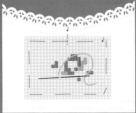

4 When the centre motif is complete, trim the surplus canvas to make room for the other motifs. Decide on the position of the next sprig, placing it a little higher if preferred to follow the curve of the neckline.

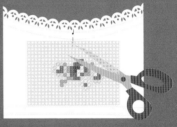

5 Cut a second piece of canvas and tack in place. Work the sprig as before. Repeat on the opposite side, so that each sprig is equidistant from the centre motif. Add the two tiny buds on the outside edges.

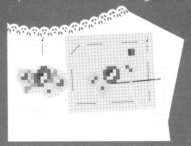

6 To dissolve the soluble canvas, carefully wash the dress in warm soapy water following the manufacturer's instructions. Rinse thoroughly, then allow to dry and iron as usual.

top tip WORK THESE VERSATILE LITTLE MOTIFS IN A CURVE AROUND A NECKLINE OR STITCH THEM SINGLY IN ROWS OR AT RANDOM ACROSS A WIDER AREA.

Lavender
Hearts

MATERIALS

• 15cm square of 14-count cross-stitch fabric • DMC stranded cotton embroidery thread in the following colours: ecru (ecru); mid-pink (603); brown (840); green (954); lilac (3042); dark pink (3804) • cross-stitch needle • 10cm square of light-weight iron-on interfacing • 15cm square of backing fabric • 30cm narrow lace edging • tracing paper and pencil • matching sewing thread • dried lavender

SKILL LEVEL: 1

No book of needlework projects is ever complete without a lavender bag! This aromatic posy sachet is a great beginner's project, which introduces some basic hand-sewing skills. It requires only a small amount of thread and fabric, so you'll have enough materials left over to make a few more for your friends.

1 Fold the cross-stitch fabric lightly into quarters to mark the centre point. The design is worked in cross stitch throughout using two strands of the embroidery thread. Following the Lavender Hearts Chart, and starting in the centre of the fabric, first work the flowers and then the leaves.

2 Trace or photocopy the heart template from the Lavender Hearts sheet, and cut it out. Place the template on to the interfacing and draw around the outside edge with a sharp pencil. Cut along the outline.

3 Position the heart centrally over the back of the completed embroidery, with the adhesive side downwards. Following the manufacturer's guidelines, iron it in place. (This will prevent the lavender working through the holes in the fabric).

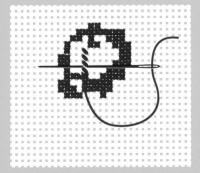

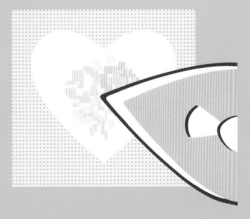

top tip CROSS-STITCH FABRIC COMES IN A RANGE OF SUBTLE PASTEL COLOURS. THIS TIME I PICKED A SOFT SKY BLUE, BUT THE FLOWERS WOULD WORK EQUALLY WELL AGAINST A BACKGROUND OF PALEST GREEN, POWDER PINK, LEMON OR IVORY.

Lavender
Hearts

4 Now tack the template directly over the interfacing and trim the cross-stitch fabric down to an 8mm margin all round. Snip into the fabric at top of the heart.

5 Turn back the margin and tack it to the template, easing it round the curves. Press from the wrong side and remove the template.

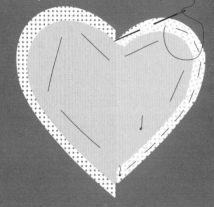

6 Fold the lace in half to find the centre. Starting with this point tucked behind the tip of the heart, slip stitch the lace along the right edge of the heart. Tuck the loose end down between the two curves at the top and stitch in place. Sew the other edge in the same way.

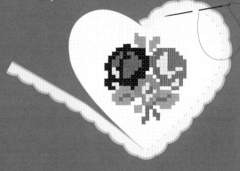

7 Tack the template to the backing fabric, then trim and tack the edges as you did before to make a neatened heart.

8 With wrong sides facing, pin and tack the front to the back.

9 Stitch together around the end, passing the needle from front to back and through the lace. Leave a 3cm opening along one edge.

10 Fill the bag with lavender, a teaspoon full at a time, pushing the dried buds right into the curves. Close the gap with neat slip stitches.

top tip THIS LAVENDER BAG IS ALMOST TOO PRETTY TO HIDE AWAY BETWEEN YOUR LINENS, BUT YOU CAN EASILY TURN IT INTO A HANGING HEART. SEW A LENGTH OF RIBBON TO THE CENTRE TOP, TIE THE ENDS TO MAKE A LOOP AND SLIP IT OVER A HOOK OR DOOR HANDLE.

Stripe
Rug

MATERIALS

• 70 x 100cm 5-count rug canvas • masking tape • DMC tapestry wool in the following colours: ecru (7271) – 30 skeins; mid-green (7384) – 10 skeins; yellow (7422) – 6 skeins; black (7538) – 5 skeins; mid-blue (7592) – 20 skeins; dark pink (7640) – 27 skeins; light pink (7804) – 7 skeins • extra large tapestry needle • 60 x 95cm linen or hessian for backing fabric • dressmaker's pins • quilting thread • large sewing needle

SKILL LEVEL: 2

This fabulous rug is a real show-stopper! After the subtle stripes of the gadget case, I wanted to try something similar but on a much larger scale – so here it is. It's not the sort of project that you'll finish in a month: you'll come back to this rug again and again, and learn some interesting new textured stitches as you go.

The Stripe Rug chart shows just one block of the repeating stripe design. Extend the length of the stripes and repeat the design as many times as necessary to cover your canvas. My rug measures approximately 50 x 92cm: I used the quantities of tapestry wool given above and repeated the block of stripes twice. You don't need to buy all the yarn at once, as any difference in the dye lots won't affect the finished appearance, so you can just get few skeins at a time and add in any extra wools you already have.

1 Bind the four edges of the canvas with masking tape.

2 Thread a large tapestry needle with a 120cm length of dark blue yarn and knot the ends together so that you are working with a double thickness to cover the canvas completely. Start stitching about 13cm diagonally in from the bottom left corner, with the short edge of the canvas facing towards you.

3 The first row of stitches, represented by the first two rows of squares on the far right-hand side of the chart, consists of 46 double cross stitches. (Instructions for double cross stitch and all the other decorative stitches used to make this rug can be found on pages 18–19 at the front of this book). The second row, represented by a single line of squares, is a line of long-armed cross stitches (see page 18) worked with a double length of ecru yarn.

4 The third row, again represented by two rows of squares, is another row of double cross stitches, this time in dark pink.

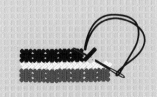

top tip WORK EACH STRIPE EITHER IN A SINGLE COLOUR OR, AS I DID, BLEND IN A FEW SKEINS OF DARKER OR LIGHTER SHADES LEFT OVER FROM OTHER PROJECTS TO GIVE THE STITCHES A RICHNESS AND DEPTH OF COLOUR: THE CLOSE-UP ON PAGES 116–17 SHOWS THIS IN DETAIL.

Stripe Rug

5 Work two rows of yellow cross stitch and another row of double cross stitch in dark pink. The next row, in sloping gobelin stitch (see page 19), is worked over two threads of the canvas using three lengths of ecru yarn. This is necessary to cover the canvas for sloping gobelin stitch only, so use three lengths each time.

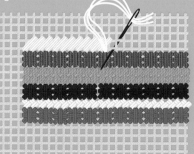

6 Continue following the chart to the end of the repeat, then start again with the first row of dark pink double cross stitch. You can copy the stitches I used as shown in the photograph on pages 116–17 or devise some variations of your own. As a guide, cross and long-armed cross stitches are worked over one canvas thread (one row of squares), double cross, sloping gobelin and plait stitches are worked over two canvas threads (two rows of squares), while a wider version of plait stitch is worked over three threads (three rows of squares).

7 Once the design is finally complete, block the canvas if necessary. Trim the excess canvas down to a 3cm margin all round. Press the corners in at 45 degress to mitre them, then press back the edges of the canvas.

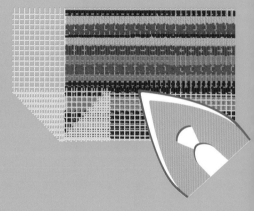

8 Press a 5cm turning all round the backing fabric. To reduce bulk, mitre the corners neatly by pressing the corners inwards, lining up the creases. Trim the tips from each of the corner triangles and then re-press the creases.

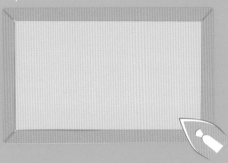

9 With wrong sides together, pin the backing fabric to the canvas, making sure that both pieces lie flat.

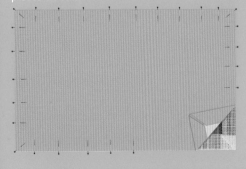

10 Stitch the canvas and backing fabric together by hand using a strong quilting thread. Work a round of slip stitches, each time taking up a single canvas thread and a few threads of the folded edge of the backing fabric.

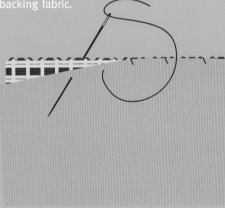

top tip SAFETY ALERT! ALWAYS PLACE A NON-SLIP UNDERLAY BENEATH YOUR RUG TO PREVENT IT SLIDING OVER A HARD SURFACE OR OUT OF PLACE ACROSS CARPETED FLOOR. AN ALTERNATIVE IS ANTI-SLIP SPRAY FINISH, WHICH IS APPLIED TO THE BACK OF THE FINISHED RUG.

Spot
Doorstop

MATERIALS

• 1 standard UK house brick or • 30 x 50cm mount board or similar weight cardboard; • roll of parcel tape; • plastic pellet toy filling • 50 x 100cm cotton or polyester wadding • matching sewing threads • sewing needle • 40 x 50cm 10-count Penelope canvas in antique • tapestry frame • DMC tapestry wools in the following colours: pink (7804) – 3 skeins; green (7911) – 14 skeins • tapestry needle • fine string • 13 x 25cm pink cotton fabric for base • iron • dressmaker's pins

SKILL LEVEL: 1

This practical doorstop is made from a humble house brick that has been transformed with a layer of padding and a vibrant needlepoint cover. The chart is designed to fit a standard UK brick, but if you don't have one to hand, you can make an alternative version from cardboard and fill it!

1 To make a 'brick' cut six pieces of card: two 6.5 x 21.5cm sides, two 10 x 6.5cm ends, and the 10 x 21.5cm lid and base. Fix the sides and ends to the base with parcel tape, then join the edges to make a box. Fill to just below the rim with the plastic pellet toy filling before adding the lid. Bind the completed 'brick' with two layers of parcel tape.

2 Wrap the wadding twice around the brick and tack down the short edge. Make four cuts into the overlap at each end, in line with the corners, so you have four flaps. Fold the lower one up and the side ones inwards. Tack down the side and bottom edges of the top flap.

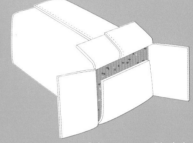

3 Mark the centre of the canvas. Bind the edges of the canvas with masking tape or mount it in a frame, if you wish.

4 The design is worked in a combination tent stitch and mosaic stitch. Following the Spot Doorstop chart, counting the squares on the chart carefully to make sure that the spots are spaced regularly, work the pink spots in tent stitch.

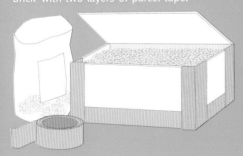

top tip TO GIVE YOUR DOORSTOP A BETTER GRIP ON THE FLOOR IN A CARPETED ROOM, ADD TWO 20CM LENGTHS OF VELCRO TO THE BASE. USE THE HOOKED SIDE AND FIX ONE STRIP TO EACH LONG EDGE OF THE BACKING BEFORE SEWING IT IN PLACE.

Spot Doorstop

5 Fill in the background with mosaic stitch (see page 19) using the green yarn. This stitch consists of small squares made up of two short and one long diagonal stitch: keep the pattern consistent by working part stitches around the dots.

6 When the design is complete, remove the canvas from the frame and block if necessary. Trim the excess canvas down to a 2cm margin all around the cross shape.

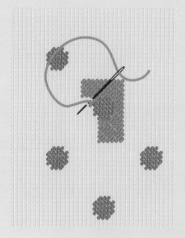

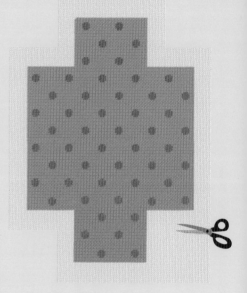

7 Turn under the canvas at one short edge, then take it across to meet the adjacent edge. Starting at the inside corner, slip stitch the two together using a double length of sewing thread. Sew to the end of the green stitching. Do the same on the other three corners and slip the cover over the brick.

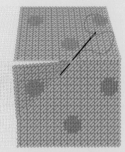

8 To create a tight, upholstered look, lace the cover in place. Thread the tapestry needle with fine string and work a series of long stitches between the two short ends. Draw them up so that the last two rows of mosaic stitch are pulled over the side to the base. Lace the two long ends together in exactly the same way.

9 Press under a 2cm turning along each edge of the fabric for the base. Pin to the underside of the doorstop, making sure that it lies centrally. Sew in place by hand using small slip stitches worked in matching sewing thread.

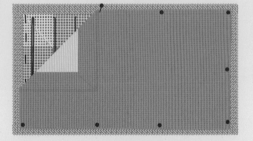

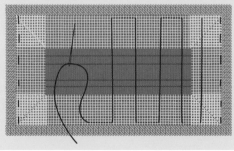

top tip I SOURCED A VIBRANT PINK COTTON FABRIC – THE PERFECT MATCH FOR THE SPOTS – TO COVER THE BASE OF THE DOORSTOP. ALTHOUGH FEW PEOPLE WILL LIEFT IT UP AND LOOK UNDERNEATH, IT'S DETAILS LIKE THIS THAT GIVE YOUR WORK A UNIQUE FINISHING TOUCH.

Sail Boat
Candleshade

MATERIALS

• linen • 11cm square soluble canvas • DMC stranded cotton embroidery thread – 1 skein in each of the following colours: white (blanc); green (320); dark blue (334); red (666); light blue (775); mid-blue (932); yellow (3822) • embroidery needle • length of ricrac equal to the bottom circumference of the shade plus 5cm • pencil • sewing machine • matching sewing thread

CUTTING OUT THE LINEN

length: Add 10cm to the bottom circumference of the shade
width: Add 5cm to the depth of the shade

SKILL LEVEL: 1

This jaunty cross-stitch yacht, surrounded by clouds, gulls and waves, gives a nautical look to a linen candleshade. Designed to slip over either a paper or metal base, this embroidered candleshade will flood your home with a flattering warm light. It almost goes without saying, but never leave a lighted candle unattended.

1 Fold the linen in half lengthways to mark the middle. Tack an 11cm square of soluble canvas centrally over this point, 2cm above the lower edge. Work two lines of tacking stitches diagonally across the canvas to make a large cross: this will give you a centre point from which to start stitching.

2 The design is worked in cross stitch throughout using two strands of the embroidery thread. Following the Sail Boat Candleshade chart, and starting in the centre of the canvas, work the yacht's dark blue masts and then the two red and yellow sails.

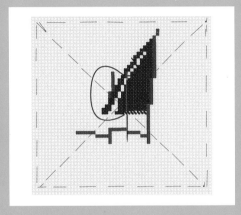

3 Continue with the green boat, then the waves in mid and light blue. Finally stitch the clouds and pennant in light blue and the gulls in dark blue.

top tip MY SAIL BOAT WORKS VERY WELL AS A SINGLE MOTIF ON THIS SMALL SCALE, BUT IF YOU WISH TO COVER A TABLE LAMPSHADE, SIMPLY ENLARGE THE BACKGROUND FABRIC AND STITCH A WHOLE FLOTILLA OF YACHTS AROUND THE LOWER EDGE.

Sail Boat
Candleshade

4 Machine stitch the two short edges of the linen together with a 1.5cm seam. Trim the seam allowance back to 5mm and carefully press the seam open. Press back a 1cm turning all round the lower edge.

5 Starting at the back seam, slip stitch the ricrac to the wrong side of the lower edge. Position it so that a series of little scallops just peep out from below the edge, echoing the cross-stitch waves. Neaten the ends as described on page 34.

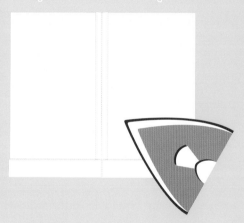

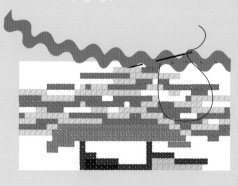

top tip FINISH OFF ALL YOUR THREADS NEATLY SO THAT NO STRAY SHADOWS SHOW THROUGH WHEN THE SHADE IS ILLUMINATED.

6 Press a 4cm hem all round the upper edge. With a sharp pencil, mark a light line all the way round, 2cm down from the fold. Thread a needle with a double length of sewing thread. Starting at the back seam, work a round of running stitches along the guideline. Work a second line of stitches, directly below the first. Leave both ends of the thread loose.

7 Draw the two loose threads up gently until the gathered linen snugly fits the top of the paper shade. Sew in both ends of the thread securely to finish.

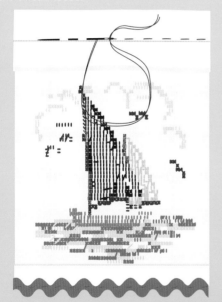

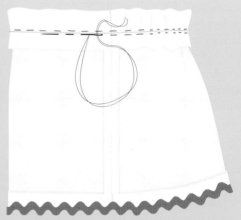

8 Turn the candleshade right side out and press lightly. Slip in place over the paper shade.

Spot
Tea Cosy

MATERIALS

• 35 x 90cm 11-count cross-stitch fabric in ecru • DMC stranded cotton embroidery thread – 1 skein in each of the following colours: lemon (165); pink (603); blue (813); green (954); coral (3705) • large cross-stitch needle • squared pattern paper or tracing paper • dressmaker's pins • sewing machine • matching sewing thread • sewing needle • 30 x 80cm heavy-weight wadding • 30 x 80cm lining fabric • 75cm matching braid • 15 x 8cm thin cardboard • pair of compasses and pencil • one 50g ball of coral cotton yarn • large tapestry needle

SKILL LEVEL: 1

The dotty design looks particularly cheerful in primary colours, so this generously sized cosy is guaranteed to brighten up your breakfast table or an afternoon tea tray. The spots are worked in all six strands of embroidery thread to create a raised appearance and the cosy is topped off with an easy-to-make pompon.

1 Cut the cross-stitch fabric in half lengthways to give two matching pieces measuring 35cm high x 45cm wide. The front and back of the tea cosy are made in exactly the same way.

2 Fold one piece of the cross-stitch fabric lightly into quarters to find the centre point. The design is worked in cross stitch throughout using all six strands of the embroidery thread. Work the cross

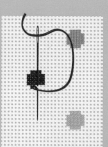

stitches either in rows or individually, for a slightly plumper look. Following the Spot Tea Cosy chart, and starting in the centre of the fabric, work the central green spot. Continue to work the design outwards, carefully counting the squares between each coloured spot. Finish each spot off neatly so that no threads show through the fabric.

3 Copy the template from the Spot Tea Cosy sheet on to squared pattern paper. Pin the template centrally to the embroidered fabric so the centre line runs through the middle row of spots and the bottom edge lies 3cm below the lowest spots. Cut out the front and back pieces in exactly the same way.

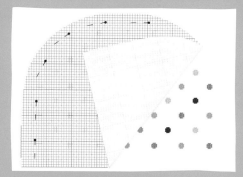

top tip TO SAVE TIME, YOU COULD USE A CO-ORDINATING FABRIC TO BACK THE TEA COSY.

REMEMBER TO HALVE YOUR QUANTITIES OF CROSS-STITCH AND BACKING FABRICS IF YOU DO.

Spot
Tea Cosy

4 With right sides facing, place the front on top of the back. Pin and tack the two together all round the curved edge, leaving the lower edge open. Stitch the edges together with a 1.5cm seam. Trim the seam allowance back to 5mm. Turn the tea cosy right side out and press lightly, using a cloth to protect the raised cross stitches. Press under a 1.5cm hem around the opening.

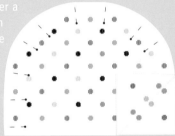

5 Using the template, cut two shapes from the wadding. Trim 2cm from the lower edge of both pieces. Pin the two together all round the curved edge. Stitch the edges together with a 2cm seam. Trim the seam allowance back to 5mm.

6 The final stage is to make the inner lining. Using the template, cut two shapes from the lining fabric. Pin the two together all round the curved edge. Stitch the edges together with a 2cm seam. Trim the seam allowance back to 5mm.

7 Press back a 2cm hem around the opening of the lining. Slip the lining inside the wadding. Tuck the lower edge of the wadding inside the hem and pin.

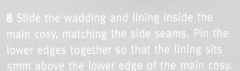

8 Slide the wadding and lining inside the main cosy, matching the side seams. Pin the lower edges together so that the lining sits 5mm above the lower edge of the main cosy. Stitch the lining to the cosy either by hand or by machine.

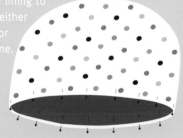

top tip POLYESTER WADDING MAKES A GOOD LIGHTWEIGHT FILLING FOR THE COSY, BUT YOU COULD BE MORE
ECO-CONSCIOUS AND RECYCLE AN OLD WOOLLY JUMPER OR BLANKET INSTEAD.

9 Sew the braid to the bottom edge of the cosy, so that the join lies along a seam line. Neaten the ends as described on page 34.

10 To make the foundation for the pompon, cut two 6cm discs of card, each with a 2cm hole in the centre. Thread a large tapestry needle with three or four lengths of yarn, about 80cm long. Hold the two discs together and pass the needle through the hole, across the back and down through the hole once again Repeat until the card is covered evenly and the centre hole filled in. Add extra lengths of yarn as you go, leaving the loose ends on the outer edge of the disc.

11 Gently push the point of your scissors under a few layers of yarn at the outer edge and snip through them. Once you have done this, you will be able to slip one blade between the two cardboard discs. Cut through the strands of yarn, all the way round the discs. The discs will keep them together.

12 Cut a length of yarn and slide it between the two discs. Pull the ends up tightly and knot securely. Remove the discs, tearing them if necessary. Trim off the long yarn ends. Roll the pompon between the palms of your hands to give it a nice round shape. Sew the pompon securely to the top of the cosy as the perfect finishing touch.

Cherry
Border

MATERIALS

- length of scalloped edging or hemmed fabric strip cut to length of shelf plus 5cm • soluble canvas
- DMC stranded cotton embroidery thread – 1 skein in each of the following colours: ecru (ecru); light green (320); dark red (355); dark green (520); red (817); pink (962) • embroidery needle • tacking thread

SKILL LEVEL: 1

This vintage border was a lucky flea market find that just needed a bit of extra embellishment... and fortunately the delectable cross-stitch cherries fitted perfectly on to the embroidered scallops. I used simple metal upholstery tacks to fix the edging onto my shelf, spacing them evenly along the top edge.

1 For each cherry motif, cut a 5cm square of soluble canvas and tack it centrally to a scallop or along the width of the fabric. If using a ready-made edging, work the motifs in the centre of the scallops. On a plain fabric, measure 8cm evenly between each cherry motif.

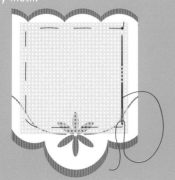

2 The design is worked in cross stitch throughout using two strands of embroidery thread. Following the Cherry Border chart, work the pink and red fruits, then the white highlights and the dark red lowlights. Add the stalks and leaves in two shades of green.

3 When the design is complete, trim away any excess soluble canvas. To dissolve the soluble canvas, carefully wash the border in warm soapy water following the manufacturer's instructions. Rinse thoroughly, then allow to dry. Once dry, press well, adding a little starch or fabric stiffener if you like. Press under the side edges and tack in place along your shelf.

top tip IF YOU AREN'T LUCKY ENOUGH TO FIND A SIMILAR SCALLOPED EDGING,

THESE CHERRIES LOOK JUST AS TASTY STITCHED ON TO A NARROW BAND OF PLAIN LINEN.

Bouquet
Seat Cover

MATERIALS

• 60cm square 10-count canvas • tapestry frame • DMC tapestry wools in the following colours: pale green (7322) – approx 24 skeins, depending on size of seat; mid-pink (7135); off-white (7141); sage green (7392) – 3 skeins each dark blue (7306); light sage (7331); brown (7938) – 1 skein each mustard yellow (7473); dark pink (7640) – 2 skeins each • tapestry needle • large sheet of paper or newspaper • pencil • tapestry needle • scissors • heavy-duty staple gun or small hammer and a box of 13mm tacks

SKILL LEVEL: 3

When you think of traditional needlepoint, a chair seat is one of the first projects that comes to mind... and quite rightly so. It is a valued investment of your time and skill, which will be enjoyed for many years. Start off with a single chair and one day you might end up with a matching set of six around your dining table!

1 To make the template, lift the seat out of the chair and place it on a large sheet of paper. Draw around the outline to give you the actual shape of the chair seat; to allow for the depth of the seat, draw a second line 3mm away from the first. If the seat is deeply padded, you may need to make this margin a little wider.

2 Cut out the template and position it centrally on the canvas. Draw all round the edge of the template on to the canvas to give the outline for your stitching.

3 The design is worked in half-cross stitch throughout. Mark the centre of the canvas. Following the Bouquet Seat Cover chart, starting from the centre of the canvas, work the three large roses. Continue to work the design outwards with the smaller flowers, leaves and buds. Fill in the background using the pale green yarn, stitching as far as the pencil line.

top tip I RE-PAINTED MY CHAIR WITH TWO COATS OF LUSTROUS GLOSS PAINT, WHICH WAS SPECIALLY MIXED TO THE SAME SHADE AS THE BRIGHTEST PINK YARN.

Bouquet
Seat Cover

4 When the design is complete, block the work if necessary. Trim the excess canvas down to a 4cm margin all round. With right sides facing, fold the canvas in half lengthways and mark the centre along each margin. Fold in half widthways and do the same.

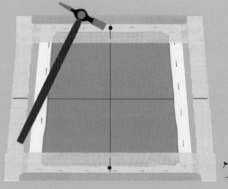

5 Turn the chair seat upside down. Mark the centre of the top and bottom edges and rule a line between the two. Measure and mark the centre of this line and draw a line across the seat at this point.

6 Place the canvas on the floor with the right side facing downwards. Position the chair seat on top, so that the pencil lines match up on each side.

7 Fold the canvas margin along the bottom edge so that 5–10mm of the stitching lies at the back. Line up the pencil marks, then hammer a tack through the canvas and into the seat. If you prefer, use a staple gun.

8 Fold back the canvas at the top, pulling it gently and tack it down. Do the same with the side edges, again pulling the canvas gently to maintain the tension.

9 Turn in the corners at 45 degree angles and tack down the canvas. Make sure that the pencil marks remain aligned.

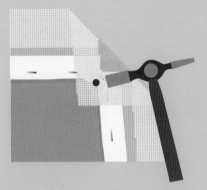

10 Fold over the canvas to one side of the corner and tack down, pulling it gently. Fix down the other side, taking care avoid the previous tack or staple.

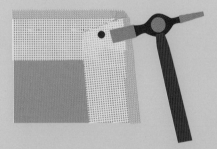

11 Continue adding tacks at 3cm intervals in the spaces between the existing tacks. Try not to pull the canvas too tightly or the edges of the seat will become uneven, but keep an even tension all the way across.

12 For a professionally neat finish, cut a piece of calico using the paper template as a guide. Press under a 3cm turning all the way round and tack or staple to the base of the seat to cover the canvas.

13 Drop the seat back in the chair when you have finished.

top tip DO TAKE CARE WHEN HAMMERING IN TACKS OR USING STAPLES, AS THEY ARE VERY SMALL, VERY SHARP AND VERY CLOSE TO YOUR FINGERTIPS!

Cowboy
Seat Cushion

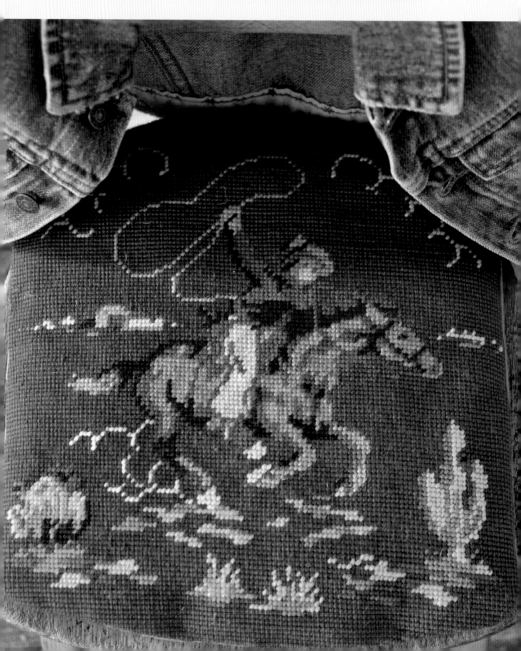

MATERIALS

• 50cm square 10-count canvas • DMC tapestry wool in the following colours: red (7758) – approx 18 skeins, depending on size of seat; blue (7029); mid-green (7384); mid-brown (7415); beige (7509); dark brown (7515) – 2 skeins each; dark cream (7141); light green (7772) – 1 skein each • sheet of paper and pencil • adhesive tape • 40cm square backing fabric • 40 x 80cm calico • polyester cushion filling • pair of brown shoelaces • sewing machine • dressmaker's pins

SKILL LEVEL: 2

My cowboy print is a perennial favourite with both children and their parents, so the exuberant Wild West horse and rider motif was a natural choice for this needlepoint kid's cushion. The finished size is 29cm wide and 31cm deep: for a smaller chair you could use a 12-count canvas to reduce the size of the design.

1 Start by making a template to fit your chair. Tape a piece of paper to the seat, at front and back, then fold it down over the edges. Draw over the crease and cut along this line. Fold the paper in half widthways and trim as necessary to make sure it is symmetrical. Double check the finished template against the seat just to be sure!

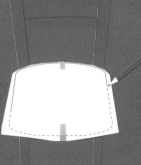

2 Fold the template in half lengthways to find the centre point. Pin the template to canvas, ensuring that it lies squarely on the weave. Draw round the outline with a pencil, then mark the middle.

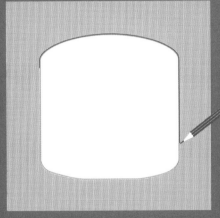

3 The design is worked in half cross stitch throughout. Following the Cowboy Seat Cushion chart, work the central cowboy. The cowboy's leg is a good starting point, next work the rest of him, followed by the horse. Count the spaces carefully to position the cactuses, lasso, clouds and other details correctly.

top tip I COULDN'T RESIST ADDING A PAIR OF OLD-FASHIONED SHOELACES TO SECURE THE CUSHION TO THE CHAIR, INSTEAD OF CONVENTIONAL FABRIC TIES.

Cowboy
Seat Cushion

4 Fill in the red background, working as far as the pencil line in each direction.

5 Once the design is complete, block the canvas if necessary. Trim the excess canvas down to a 2cm margin (the seam allowance) all round the design.

6 Pin the cushion front, right sides facing, to the backing panel. Cut along the outside edge of the canvas so that both pieces are the same size. Machine stitch the two together, leaving a 15cm opening along the top edge.

7 Press back the seam allowance (including the parts that run along the opening) at front and back. Ease it gently around the corners using a small burst of steam from the iron to set the curve. Turn the cushion right side out through the opening.

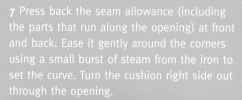

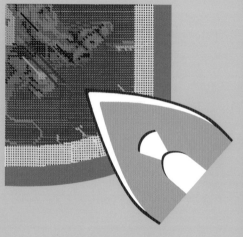

top tip THE CUSHION IS BACKED WITH A BLUE FURNISHING WEIGHT COTTON:

SALVAGED DENIM FROM AN OLD PAIR OF JEANS WOULD BE A GOOD ALTERNATIVE.

8 Make a specially shaped filling pad for the cushion, following the directions on page 32. Use the paper template as your guide, and add an extra 1cm all round when cutting out the two pieces of calico.

9 Insert the pad through the opening at the top edge. Pin the two sides of the opening together and hand stitch to close.

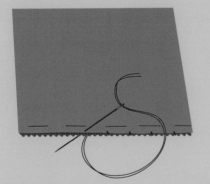

10 Place the finished cushion on the chair seat and mark the two points where it touches the back struts with pins. Fold one of the shoelaces in half and make an overhand knot at the centre. Stitch this knot securely to one of the marked points, then add the other lace in the same way.

11 Sew your braid to the cushion by hand with matching sewing thread. Use small slip stitches and line the bottom edge up along the seam line as you go. Gather the braid slightly at the corners and finish off the ends as described on page 34. Here you will also find instructions for machine stitching the braid to the cushion.

House
Picture

MATERIALS

• 35cm square 14-count cross-stitch fabric in oatmeal • DMC stranded cotton embroidery thread in the following colours: red (309) – 2 skeins; off-white (543); green (562); shell pink (758); blue (826); coral (3705); mid-pink (3731); brown (3858) – 1 skein each • cross-stitch needle • 20cm square mount board • picture frame with 20cm square opening • strong sewing thread • sewing needle

SKILL LEVEL: 2

Home Sweet Home! This appealing little house is reminiscent of traditional samplers, but the bright red roof and spotty curtains at the windows give it an unmistakably contemporary look. It is worked on unbleached cross-stitch fabric, which adds colour to the wall – and saves a lot of extra sewing!

1 Mark the centre of the cross-stitch fabric and mount it in a frame. The design is worked in cross stitch throughout using two strands of the embroidery thread. Following the House Picture chart, and starting in the centre of the fabric, first work the brown outline of the door and portico, the step, studs and door handle.

2 Using the coral thread, stitch the letterbox within the door, then fill in the triangle within the portico and the stitches between the steps and the path. Using the blue thread, fill in the door, working carefully around the brown stitches.

3 Count outwards from the door to find the correct position for the frames and sills of the two downstairs windows, which are worked in brown. Add the stitches for the glazing bars. Work the flower petals in coral and shell pink, then the leaves in green. Work the both dots of the curtains and the window panes in off-white.

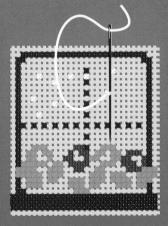

House Picture

4 Using mid-pink thread, work the curtains and the centres of the flowers, again, stitching carefully around the dots and the plants so that you don't split the thread.

6 Count upwards from the top windows and stitch the brown edging to the roof. Then work the roof in dark red – this may take some time! – and the narrow triangles of sky in blue. Finish off by sewing the red flowers in the bushes at the front and then the green bushes themselves.

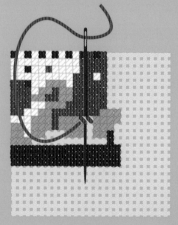

5 Count upwards from the downstairs windows to find the correct position for the upstairs windows. Work in the same way as the downstairs windows.

7 When the design is complete, remove the finished piece from the frame and press lightly from the wrong side. Trim the fabric down to a 3cm margin all round.

top tip THE MOUNTING BOARD SHOULD BE THE SAME COLOUR AS THE CROSS-STITCH FABRIC TO PREVENT ANY COLOUR SHOWING THROUGH THE HOLES.

8 The best way to mount your completed embroidery is to stitch it over a piece of board. Draw two centre lines across the back of the mount board to divide it into equal quarters. Lay the finished picture face downwards on a flat surface and position the mount board centrally on the back, so that the tacking lines match up with the pencil marks.

9 Thread a needle with a long length of strong thread. Fold the edges of the fabric inwards. Fasten the thread the centre point of one edge of the fabric, then make a long stitch across the card to the opposite edge. Continue lacing outwards, as far as the edge of the mount board, then lace from the centre to the other side.

10 Check that the sides are parallel by making sure that the lines of holes in the cross-stitch fabric lie along the edges of the board: adjust the lacing if not. Lace the other two sides in the same way. Finally fix your mounted picture in the frame.

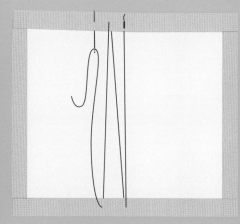

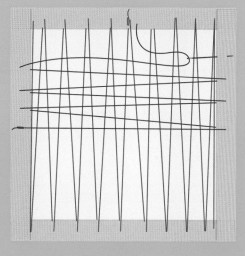

Cowboy Picture

MATERIALS

• embroidery frame • 40 x 45cm 11-count cross-stitch fabric in ecru • DMC stranded cotton embroidery thread in the following colours: red (321); blue (334); dark brown (838); light brown (841); dark green (986); light green (3364); mid-brown (3772) – 2 skeins each; off-white (3866) – 1 skein • small tapestry needle • graph paper and pencil • picture frame • mount board, cut to fit aperture in frame • strong sewing thread • sewing needle

SKILL LEVEL: 2

Generations of children learnt to sew by working fine cross-stitch samplers, complete with an improving motto. Nowadays samplers are usually made to commemorate a birth or other family event: you'll find an alphabet overleaf so that you can personalise your own version of this timeless cowboy picture.

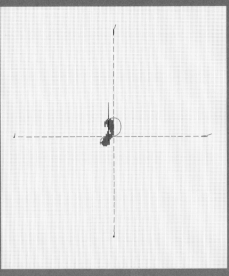

1 Mark the centre of the cross-stitch fabric and mount it in a frame. The design is worked in cross stitch throughout using all six strands of the embroidery thread, which gives the stitches a raised appearance. Following the Cowboy Picture chart, and starting in the centre of the fabric, work the cowboy's leg in blue.

2 Stitching outwards, work the cowboy and horse. Counting carefully, work the lasso, clouds, buildings and cactuses.

top tip IF YOU WANT TO INCLUDE A COMPLETE NAME OR A SHORT MESSAGE,
ADD AN EXTRA 10CM OR MORE TO THE DEPTH OF THE FABRIC.

Cowboy Picture

3 Draw up your monogram and date on graph paper, leaving a one-square gap between the characters and adding a single stitch as a full-stop after any initials. Fold the paper in half to find the centre: this corresponds with the marks on the fabric. Embroider the letters and numbers either side of this point.

4 When the design is complete, remove the finished piece from the frame and press lightly from the wrong side. Trim the fabric down to a 3cm margin all round.

5 Draw two centre lines across the back of the mount board to divide it into equal quarters. Lay the finished picture face downwards on a flat surface and position the mount board centrally on the back, so that the tacking lines match up with the pencil marks.

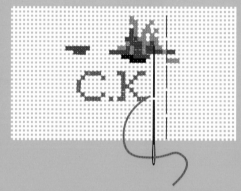

top tip IF YOU'D PREFER A COLOURED BACKGROUND, LIKE THE NEEDLEPOINT COWBOY ON PAGE 136, USE A RED CROSS-STITCH FABRIC AND CHANGE HIS SHIRT TO A BLUE DENIM SHADE.

6 Thread a needle with a long length of strong thread. Fold the edges of the fabric inwards. Fasten the thread the centre point of one edge of the fabric, then make a long stitch across the card to the opposite edge. Continue lacing outwards, as far as the edge of the mount board, then lace from the centre to the other side.

7 Check that the sides are parallel by making sure that the lines of holes in the cross-stitch fabric lie along the edges of the board: adjust the lacing if not. Lace the other two sides in the same way. FInally fix your mounted picture in the frame.

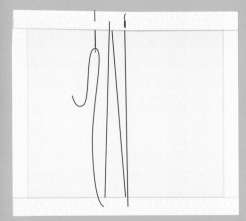

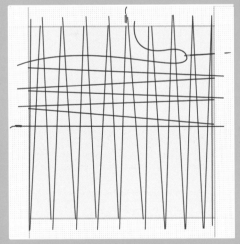

Glossary

Like other crafts, sewing, needlepoint and cross stitch have their own technical vocabulary so you may come across a few unfamiliar words. Here are the most common terms, many of which are explained further in the introductory pages.

Aida cloth The threads of this easy-to-use cross-stitch fabric are woven in square blocks, separated by holes. This creates a grid pattern that is easy to follow when you are counting the stitches.

Bargello Also known as Byzantine Work, a geometric needlepoint technique worked in upright stitches on mono canvas, following a coloured chart.

Bias grain This is found by drawing a line at a 45 degree angle to the selvedge, or straight woven edge, of the fabric. Because it lies across the straight lengthwise and crosswise grain, a fabric strip cut along the cross, or bias grain, will have a lot of stretch or 'give'.

Blocking Needlepoint stitches can often pull the canvas weave out of shape: this describes the process of restoring the stitched canvas to its original square or rectangle.

Calico Unbleached cotton calico fabric is useful for making cushion pads.

Canvas Available in three types – mono, interlock and duo – and in a range of sizes, this foundation fabric is used for all needlepoint.

Count Count (or mesh) refers to the number of holes per inch, in needlepoint and cross stitch fabrics, which determines size of the stitches. The higher the count the smaller the stitches will be.

Envelope backing A simple way to back a cushion, made up of two overlapping panels. You can add buttons and buttonholes if you wish.

Evenweave Fabric woven from warp and weft threads of similar dimensions.

Grain Fabric consists of two sets of interwoven threads, which go from top to bottom (the warp) and from side to side (the weft). The warp grain runs the length of a piece of fabric, from the top to bottom. Always cut fabric along the grain.

Gusset A narrow piece of fabric used to reinforce or to give depth to a cushion.

Hem A fabric edge that is turned under to the wrong side and stitched in place.

Interfacing Available in sew-in and iron-on versions, this is a soft non-woven fabric used to give strength and body to a light-weight material.

Lengthways As in 'fold lengthways': fold parallel to the longer edge of a piece of fabric.

Linen A natural fabric, woven from flax threads. Vintage linen sheets can be re-used as cushion backings and have a wonderfully soft textures.

Masking tape A flexible, easily removed adhesive paper tape used by decorators. Use 2.5cm wide tape to bind the rough edges of needlepoint canvas and to stop it fraying.

Pattern paper Produced in large sheets, printed with a grid of inches or centimetres, this paper is used for drawing up full-size pattern pieces.

Piping cord A fine, loosely twisted cotton 'rope' available in different thicknesses. It is covered with a bias strip of fabric to make piping.

Plush/pile Velvet and carpet both have a pile – a soft surface made up of many short cut threads. The pile causes the colour of the fabric to vary from different angles, so if you are using two pieces of velvet, always make sure the pile lies in the same direction for both.

Ply A ply is an individual strand of thread. There are six plies in embroidery thread, which can be used together or separated out and regrouped for finer stitches. Tapestry wool is made up of four loosely twisted plies that are worked together.

Press seam open Use the tip of an iron to separate the two seam allowances. Press along the line so one seam allowance lies on each side of the stitches.

Rug canvas The largest scale canvas available with a count of 5 stitches. It is used for needlepoint mats.

Scroll frame An adjustable four-sided wooden frame with rotating top and bottom struts, useful for working larger projects.

Seam The line along which two fabric edges are stitched together.

Seam allowance The distance between the cut edge of the fabric and the line of stitching.

Selvedge The woven edges of a fabric. The grain of the fabric lies parallel to the selvedge.

Size A stiffening agent, commonly used to make canvas fibres rigid.

Slip stitch This creates an unobtrusive seam, made by stitching alternately through the edges of two pieces of fabric, either along an opening or a hem.

Soluble canvas A temporary canvas for working counted cross stitch on non-evenweave fabrics.

Stab stitch Made by passing the needle through at right angles; these tiny stitches appear as small dots on the fabric's surface. Use to sew through thick layers.

Stretcher frame A rigid wooden frame on to which canvas or cross stitch fabric is pinned to maintain tension. The frame is the same size as the fabric.

Tacking Also called basting, these are easily unpicked stitches about 1.5cm long, used to hold two fabric edges together before seaming. Use tacking to mark the centre of your background fabric.

Tapestry needles Blunt, round ended needles with large eyes, which pass easily through the holes in canvas or cross stitch fabric.

Tapestry yarn A soft 4-ply wool used for needlepoint, which is available in a wide spectrum of colours.

Tension Canvas and cross-stitch fabric should be stretched tight, or kept under tension, in a frame for the best results. The term also refers to the degree of tightness in the stitches and varies according to how the yarn or thread is pulled – always keep an even tension when stitching.

Ticking A strong, striped cotton fabric with a diagonal weave used for pillow pads and mattress covers. Look out for vintage ticking, in unique striped designs.

Turn through The process of turning a finished item right sides out, through an opening in one seam. Ease the seams out and push the corners into points with a blunt pencil.

Wadding Also called batting, this is a thick, non-woven cotton or polyester fabric used to give depth and thickness. It is used pad bags and quilts.

Widthways Fold in half widthways: fold parallel to the shorter side of the fabric.

Colour Conversions

Each tapestry yarn or embroidery thread manufacturer has their own palette of colours, and use different dyes to produce each shade. This means that the alternative numbers given below are equivalents rather than exact matches. I recommend using yarn or thread from only one manufacturer for each project, rather than mixing threads from more than one source. Also, remember to check the meterage of the skeins. In this book, the number of skeins given in the materials list for each project is based on a skein containing 8m of yarn or thread.

Bargello Cushion (pages 38–41)

tapestry yarn	DMC	ANCHOR
white	blanc	8002
yellow	7049	8092 or 8112
red	7106	8212 or 8214
pink	7202	8412
green	7386	9006 or 9020
fawn	7411	–
blue	7802	8788 or 8818

Spot Cushion (pages 42–45)

tapestry yarn	DMC	ANCHOR
red	7106	8212 or 8214
off-white	7510	9052
blue	7555	–

Provence Rose Pillow (pages 46–49)

embroidery thread	DMC	ANCHOR	MADEIRA
mid-green	562	205	1213
light green	564	219	1211
light blue	747	158	1104
light pink	963	73	502
coral	3705	28	214
light coral	3706	27	303
light cream	3865	2	2403

Union Jack Cushion (pages 50–53)

tapestry yarn	DMC	ANCHOR
dark red	7108	8218 or 8442
mid-pink	7223	8506
beige	7230	9674
green	7391	8048 or 9332
yellow	7455	9524
grey-blue	7705	8720 or 9766
dark pink	7758	8400

Spray Flower Cushion (pages 54–57)

embroidery thread	DMC	ANCHOR	MADEIRA
light pink	604	50	613
light gold	676	942	2013
light green	772	259	2205
ecru	842	388	2109
mid-pink	899	27	414
green	992	1070	1110
dark pink	3350	896	604
turquoise	3766	161	1106
brown	3857	1050	2008

Colour Conversions

House Cushions (pages 58–61)

tapestry yarn	DMC	ANCHOR
ecru	ecru	8004, 8006, 8032 or 8292
pink	7004	8394 or 8432
pinky-red	7106	8212 or 8214
dark cream	7141	9482
dark blue	7306	8792
mid-green	7386	9006 or 9020
yellow	7472	8018
dark green	7541	–
dark red	7544	8216
brown	7622	9796
red	7666	8200
light green	7771	9096, 9098 or 9164
mid-blue	7802	8788 or 8818

Electric Flower Cushion (pages 62–65)

tapestry yarn	DMC	ANCHOR
mid-pink	7135	–
dark pink	7136	–
dark blue	7287	–
green	7406	9078
yellow	7470	8016
off-white	7510	9052
light blue	7594	8734 or 8832

Bargello Hippie Bag (pages 66–69)

tapestry yarn	DMC	ANCHOR
light blue	7294	8834
orange	7303	–
off-white	7331	9056 or 9064
dark blue	7336	8794
yellow	7485	8024, 8044 or 8102
brown	7515	9662
green	7541	–

Spray Clutch Bag (pages 70–73)

tapestry yarn	DMC	ANCHOR
mid-pink	7195	8368
light pink	7221	8504
dark blue	7296	–
light green	7376	9174, 9176 or 9262
dark green	7396	–
dark cream	7411	–
dark brown	7432	9624
gold	7494	9404, 9424 or 9426
dark pink	7758	8400
teal green	7927	–

Sail Boat Beach Bag (pages 74–77)

embroidery thread	DMC	ANCHOR	MADEIRA
dark red	498	1005	2502
red	817	39	507
blue-green	926	235	1703
dark blue-green	930	922	1707

Bouquet Knitting Bag (pages 78–81)

embroidery thread	DMC	ANCHOR	MADEIRA
lime green	166	279	1308
olive green	830	889	2112
red	891	35	214
pink	956	33	409
light orange	977	363	2307
brown	3031	905	1904
pale green	3348	254	1501
beige	3782	388	1906

Union Jack Purse (pages 82–85)

tapestry yarn	DMC	ANCHOR
yellow	7504	8020
off-white	7510	9052
dark pink	7603	8454 or 8456
light pink	7605	–
red	7666	8200
blue	7802	8788 or 8818
green	7911	8988 or 9118

Stanley Pencil Case (pages 86–89)

tapestry yarn	DMC	ANCHOR
beige	7520	–
tan	7525	–
black	7624	9768 or 9798
grey	7626	9764
red	7666	8200

Stripe Gadget Case (pages 90–93)

embroidery thread	DMC	ANCHOR	MADEIRA
light blue	164	1042	1210
lemon	677	300	2207
beige	822	1011	1908
coral	893	27	303
light green	927	849	1701
pink	3326	36	2605
dark blue	3768	400	1704

Electric Flower Specs Case (pages 94–97)

embroidery thread	DMC	ANCHOR	MADEIRA
red	349	35	410
green	469	681	1602
off-white	648	900	1709
yellow	733	280	2111
purple	915	65	706
pink	3805	38	413
lilac	3835	99	1808

Motif Badges (pages 98–99)

embroidery thread	DMC	ANCHOR	MADEIRA
light pink	151	73	502
light green	503	875	2604
turquoise	598	1092	1101
yellow	676	942	2013
mid-brown	841	378	1906
dark beige	3033	880	1907
dark pink	3731	1024	610
red	3801	35	410
mid-green	3848	189	1108
brown	3857	1050	2008
off-white	3865	2	2403

Provence Rose Pincushion (pages 100–103)

tapestry yarn	DMC	ANCHOR
white	blanc	8002
light green	7369	9016
dark green	7386	9006 or 9020
light pink	7605	–
red	7666	8200
light blue	7802	8788 or 8818
mid-pink	7804	8452

Colour Conversions

Little Bunch Dungarees *(pages 104–105)*

embroidery thread	DMC	ANCHOR	MADEIRA
blue	322	131	1004
dark pink	602	41	506
light pink	819	271	2314
brown	840	393	1913
green	912	205	1212
red	3801	35	410

Sprig Border Dress *(pages 106–107)*

embroidery thread	DMC	ANCHOR	MADEIRA
ecru	ecru	2	2101
green	368	241	1307
lemon	445	802	2207
dark pink	892	28	214
pink	894	36	504
light blue	3753	1037	2504

Lavender Hearts *(pages 108–111)*

embroidery thread	DMC	ANCHOR	MADEIRA
ecru	ecru	2	2101
mid-pink	603	62	414
brown	840	393	1913
green	954	203	1201
lilac	3042	676	807
dark pink	3804	54	611

Stripe Rug *(pages 112–117)*

tapestry yarn	DMC	ANCHOR
ecru	7271	–
mid-green	7384	–
yellow	7422	–
black	7538	–
mid-blue	7592	8836
dark pink	7640	–
light pink	7804	8452

Spot Doorstop *(pages 118–121)*

tapestry yarn	DMC	ANCHOR
pink	7804	8452
green	7911	8988 or 9118

Sail Boat Candleshade *(pages 122–125)*

embroidery thread	DMC	ANCHOR	MADEIRA
white	blanc	1037	2504
green	320	215	1212
dark blue	334	977	910
red	666	1098	411
light blue	775	158	1104
mid-blue	932	1033	1710
yellow	3822	288	110

Spot Tea Cosy *(pages 126–129)*

embroidery thread	DMC	ANCHOR	MADEIRA
lemon	165	293	103
pink	603	62	414
blue	813	140	909
green	954	203	1201
coral	3705	28	214

Cherry Border *(pages 130–131)*

embroidery thread	DMC	ANCHOR	
ecru	ecru	2	2101
light green	320	215	1212
dark red	355	884	2304
dark green	520	862	1514
red	817	39	507
pink	962	27	414

Bouquet Seat Cover *(pages 132–135)*

tapestry yarn	DMC	ANCHOR
mid-pink	7135	–
off-white	7141	9482
dark blue	7306	8792
light green	7322	8874 or 8894
grey	7331	9056 or 9064
green	7392	–
yellow	7473	8042
dark pink	7640	–
brown	7938	–

Cowboy Seat Cushion *(pages 136–139)*

tapestry yarns	DMC	ANCHOR
blue	7029	–
dark cream	7141	9482
mid-green	7384	–
mid-brown	7415	9368 or 9392
beige	7509	9654 or 9656
dark brown	7515	9662
red	7758	8400
light green	7772	9172

House Picture *(pages 140–143)*

embroidery thread	DMC	ANCHOR	MADEIRA
red	309	42	507
off-white	543	933	305
green	562	205	1213
shell pink	758	336	2313
blue	826	176	910
coral	3705	28	214
mid-pink	3731	1024	610
brown	3858	936	2311

Cowboy Picture *(pages 144–157)*

embroidery thread	DMC	ANCHOR	MADEIRA
red	321	42	507
blue	334	977	910
dark brown	838	905	1904
light brown	841	378	1906
dark green	986	878	1514
light green	3364	859	1401
mid-brown	3772	679	402
off-white	3866	2	2403

Addresses

Needlecraft shops

Burford Needlecraft
150 High Street
Burford
Oxfordshire OX18 4QU
01993 822 136
www.needlework.co.uk

Cross Stitch Centre
16 Fenkle Street
Alnwick
Northumberland NE66 1HR
01670 511 241
www.cross-stitch-centre.co.uk

Sew and So
Unit 8a
Chalford Industrial Estate
Chalford
Stroud
Gloucestershire GL6 8NT
01453 889 988
www.sewandso.co.uk

The Needlecraft Shop
225 Mellis Road
Thornham Parva
Eye
Suffolk IP23 8ET
01379 679 486
www.theneedlecraftshop.co.uk

Haberdasheries and fabric shops

Bedecked
5 Castle Street
Hay-on-Wye
Hereford HR3 5DF
01497 822 769
www.bedecked.co.uk

Christie Bears
2 Mill Barn
Mill Road
Boverton
Llantwit Major
South Glamorgan CF61 1UB
01446 790 090
www.christiebears.co.uk

Deckchair Stripes
PO Box 273
Tarporley
Cheshire CW6 9XZ
0845 500 1005 or 01829 734 077
www.deckchairstripes.com

Cloth House
47 Berwick Street
London W1F 8SJ
020 7437 5155
www.clothhouse.net

John Lewis
Oxford Street
London W1A 1EX
and branches nationwide
08456 049 049
www.johnlewis.com

Merrick & Day
Redbourne Road
Redbourne
Gainsborough
Lincolnshire DN21 4TG
01652 648 814
www.merrick-day.com

Harts of Hertford
14 Bull Plain
Hertford SG14 1DT
01992 558 106
www.hartsofhertford.com

Mandors
134 Renfrew Street
Glasgow G3 6ST
0141 332 7716
www.mandors.co.uk

MacCulloch & Wallis
25–26 Dering Street
London W1S 1AT
020 7629 0311
www.macculloch-wallis.co.uk

Millie Moon
20 Paul Street
Frome
Somerset BA11 1DT
01373 464 650
www.milliemoonshop.co.uk

Peabees Patchwork Bazaar
1 Hare Street
Sheerness
Kent ME12 1AH
01795 669 963
www.peabees.com

Rags
19 Chapel Walk
Crowngate Shopping Centre
Worcester WR1 3LD
01905 612 330

Sew and So's
14 Upper Olland Street
Bungay
Suffolk NR35 1BG
01986 896 147
www.sewandsos.co.uk

Tikki
293 Sandycombe Road
Kew
Surrey TW9 3LU
020 8948 8462
www.tikkilondon.com

Needlepoint Classes

All Stitched Up
Errington House
Humshaugh
Hexham
Northumberland NE46 4HP
01434 672 389
www.needle-point.co.uk

Tapisserie
54 Walton Street
London SW3 1RB
020 7581 2715
www.tapisserie.co.uk

Sewing Classes

Liberty Sewing School
Regent Street
London W1B 5AH
020 7734 1234
www.liberty.co.uk

The Makery
146 Walcott Street
Bath BA1 5BL
01225 421 175
www.themakeryonline.co.uk

The Papered Parlour
7 Prescott Place
London SW4 6BS
020 7627 8703
www.thepaperedparlour.co.uk

Sue Hazell Sewing Tuition
Southcombe House
Chipping Norton
Oxfordshire OX7 5QH
www.sewing-tuition.co.uk

The Studio London
Studio 5
Trinity Buoy Wharf
64 Orchard Place
London E14 0JW
www.thestudiolondon.co.uk

A few handy websites:

DMC Creative World
www.dmccreative.co.uk
For stockists of DMC stranded
cotton and tapestry wool.

Elliot Anti-Slip
www.antislip.biz
Anti-slip underlay, tape and spray
to prevent rugs slipping on tiled or
wooden floors.

Etsy
www.etsy.com
An online marketplace for
everything handmade and vintage,
including
fabric and other sewing supplies.

Ribbon Moon
www.ribbonmoon.co.uk
For ricrac and bias binding in a
wide range of colours and widths.

Cath Kidston Stores

Bath
3 Broad Street
Milsom Place
Bath BA1 5LJ
01225 331 006

Bicester Village Outlet Store
Unit 21
Bicester Village
Bicester OX26 6WD
01869 247 358

Birmingham – Selfridges
Upper Mall
East Bullring
Birmingham B5 4BP
0121 600 6967

Bluewater
Unit Loo3, Rose Gallery
Blue Water Shopping Centre
DA9 9SH
01322 387 454

Brighton
31a & 32 East Street
Brighton BN1 1HL
01273 227 420

Bristol
79 Park Street
Clifton
Bristol BS1 5PF
0117 930 4722

Cambridge
31–33 Market Hill
Cambridge CB2 3NU
01223 351 810

Canterbury
6 The Parade
Canterbury CT1 2JL
01227 455 639

Cardiff
45 The Hayes
St David's
Cardiff CF10 1GA
02920 225 627

Cheltenham
21 The Promenade
Cheltenham GL50 1LE
01242 245 912

Chichester
24 South Street
Chichester PO19 1EL
01243 850 100

Dublin
Unit CSD 1.3
Dundrum Shopping Centre
Dublin 16
00 353 1 296 4430

Edinburgh
58 George Street
Edinburgh EH2 2LR
0131 220 1509

Glasgow
18 Gordon Street
Glasgow G1 3PB
0141 248 2773

Guildford
14–18 Chertsey Street
Guildford GU1 4HD
01483 564 798

Gunwharf Quays Outlet Store
Gunwharf Quays
Portsmouth PO1 3TU
02392 832 982

Harrogate
2–6 James Street
Harrogate HG1 1RF
01423 531 481

Heathrow Terminal 4
Departure Lounge
Heathrow Airport TW6 3XA
020 8759 5578

Kildare Village Outlet Store
Unit 21c Kildare Village
Nurney Road
Kildare Town
00 353 45 535 084

Kingston
10 Thames Street
Kingston Upon Thames KT1 1PE
020 8546 6760

Leeds
26 Lands Lane
Leeds LS1 6LB
0113 391 2692

Liverpool
Compton House
18 School Lane
Liverpool L1 3BT
0151 709 2747

London – Battersea
142 Northcote Road
London SW11 6RD
020 7228 6571

London – Chiswick
125 Chiswick High Road
London W4 2ED
020 8995 8052

London – Covent Garden
28–32 Shelton Street
London WC2H 9JE
020 7836 4803

London – Fulham
668 Fulham Road
London SW6 5RX
020 7731 6531

London – Kings Road
322 Kings Road
London SW3 5UH
020 7351 7335

London – Marylebone
51 Marylebone High Street
London W1U 5HW
020 7935 6555

London – Notting Hill
158 Portobello Road
London W11 2BE
020 7727 5278

London – Selfridges
Oxford Street
London W1A 1AB
020 7318 3312

London – Sloane Square
27 Kings Road
London SW3 4RP
020 3463 4840

London – St Pancras
St Pancras International Station
Pancras Road
London NW1 2Qp
020 7837 4125

London – Wimbeldon Village
3 High Street
Wimbledon
London SW19 5DX
020 8944 1001

Manchester
62 King Street
Manchester M2 4ND
0161 834 7936

Manchester – Selfridges
1 Exchange Square
Manchester M3 1BD
0161 838 0610

Manchester – Selfridges
1 The Dome
Trafford Centre
Manchester M17 8DA
0161 629 1184

Marlborough
142–142a High Street
Marlborough SN8 1HN
01672 512 514

Marlow
6 Market Square
Marlow SL7 1DA
01628 484 443

Newcastle – Fenwicks
Lower Ground Floor
Northumberland Street
Newcastle Upon Tyne NE99 1AR
0191 232 5100

Oxford
6 Broad Street
Oxford OX1 3AJ
01865 791 576

St Ives
67 Fore Street
St Ives TR26 1HE
01736 798 001

St Neots Factory Store
1a Alpha Drive
Eaton Socon
St Neots PE19 8JJ
01480 473 175

Tunbridge Wells
59–61 High Street
Tunbridge Wells TN1 1XU
01892 521 197

Winchester
46 High Street
Winchester SO23 9BT
01962 870 620

Windsor
24 High Street
Windsor SL4 1LH
01753 830 591

York
32 Stonegate
York YO1 8AS
01904 733 653

Acknowledgements

Many thanks to Lucinda Ganderton and her team of lady stitchers: Karen Belton, Shirley Cross, Jane Fowler, Lis Gunner, Alison Hadfield, Sandra Hubbard, Phyllis Johnson, Sheila Meen, Lynda Potter, Jen Russell and Janice Spooner for making all of the projects; and to Pia Tryde, Laura Mackay, Elisabeth Lester, Elaine Ashton and Caroline Bell. Thanks also to Helen Lewis, Lisa Pendreigh, Katherine Case and Bridget Bodoano at Quadrille.

Cath Kidston

Series Creative Coordinator: Elaine Ashton
Design Assistant to Cath Kidston: Laura Mackay
Stitching Coordinator and Consultant: Lucinda Ganderton

Editorial Director: Anne Furniss
Art Director: Helen Lewis
Project Editor: Lisa Pendreigh
Designer: Katherine Case
Photographer: Pia Tryde
Illustrator: Bridget Bodoano
Production Director: Vincent Smith
Production Controller: Aysun Hughes

Quadrille *craft*

www.quadrillecraft.co.uk

If you have any comments or queries regarding the instructions in this book, please contact us at enquiries@quadrille.co.uk.

This edition published in 2012 by
Quadrille Publishing Limited
Alhambra House
27–31 Charing Cross Road
London WC2H 0LS

First published in 2010
Text copyright © Cath Kidston 2010
Design templates and projects © Cath Kidston 2010
Photography © Pia Tryde 2010
Design and layout copyright © Quadrille Publishing Limited 2010

The rights of Cath Kidston to be identified as the author of this work have been asserted in accordance with the Copyright, Design and Patents Act 1988.

Cataloguing-in-Publication Data: a catalogue record for this book is available from the British Library.

ISBN 978 184949 139 6

Printed in China